MW00698971

Adams Media
An Imprint of Simon & Schuster, Inc.
100 Technology Center Drive
Stoughton, Massachusetts 02072

First Adams Media hardcover edition April 2022

ADAMS MEDIA and colophon are trademarks of Simon & Schuster.

For information about special discounts for bulk purchases, please
contact Simon & Schuster Special Sales at 1-866-506-1949 or
business@simonandschuster.com.

The Simon & Schuster Speakers Bureau can bring authors to your live
event. For more information or to book an event contact the Simon
& Schuster Speakers Bureau at 1-866-248-3049 or visit our website at
www.simonspeakers.com.

Interior design, illustrations, and hand lettering by Priscilla Yuen

Manufactured in the United States of America

1 2022

ISBN 978-1-5072-1825-9

To Lalo, Lalu, and Fifi.

ACKNOWLEDGMENTS

This book was a labor of love made easier by a wonderful support system—and the blessing of Mercury in Virgo conjunct the Ascendant. (That's on you, Mom and Dad.) Thank you to my favorite people in the world: the Triquetra and Sofia Maria. Thank you to the wonderful team at Adams Media: Rebecca Tarr Thomas for believing in me, Sarah Doughty for making this book better, and Julia DeGraf for her sharp eye. I would like to thank the Fairfield University MFA Creative Writing program, especially Nick Mancuso, Mary Lide, Rachel Basch, Sonya Huber, and the late Da Chen. I am so honored that I am asked to share my insights with *Well+Good* readers, and for that I must thank Mary Grace Garis and Erica Sloan. I am blessed in this lifetime with the most supportive friends: Thank you for encouraging me about my passion, even when you didn't understand it. Thank you to my astro-community of fellow spiritual enthusiasts, stargazers, and tarot lovers, especially Stephanie Powell, Annabel Gat, Thea Anderson, and Sam Reynolds. Finally, thank you to my teachers and guides—the ones in this physical realm and the ones beyond.

Contents

◉ INTRODUCTION ◉

Do you wonder how you can connect with the Universe? How to filter out the noise and really listen to the wisdom inside yourself? Or how to trust that intuitive understanding when you hear it?

The One Card Tarot Journal is your guide to tapping in to the secrets of the Universe—and of your own mind— with just one card. There are no elaborate tarot spreads to unpack here. No tarot "experts" intimidating you into confusing interpretations that don't resonate with you. Instead, you will use the one card spread (and any tarot deck you choose) to access the power of your own intuition. Each card drawn in a tarot deck holds insightful messages. And by connecting those messages to your unique experiences, you will learn how to listen to the wisdom of not just the world around you, but also within yourself.

In Part 1, you'll explore the essentials of tarot, from the benefits of a daily one card practice, including grounding yourself in the present and keeping things simple, to common misconceptions about the cards. Then you'll learn how to complete the one card spread in three easy steps:

1 Set an intention for what you are hoping to manifest and the guidance you seek from tarot.
2 Shuffle the deck as you focus on your intention.
3 Draw a card and meditate on how it connects to your life experiences and desires.

In Part 2, it will be your turn to take charge of the cards. Here, you'll find 150 guided prompts to help you interpret the messages of different one card spreads. Additionally, there are forty-five open-ended prompts that will guide you to answer your own yes or no questions. This part is organized by theme, so you'll use tarot to examine self-care, your relationships with others and yourself, your career and finances, your health, your spiritual development, and the specific questions you want answered.

Not sure what a reversed Hanged Man means? Can't remember the traditional wisdom of the Nine of Cups? Part 3 is your guide to the meanings and associations for each tarot card you draw. Flip forward to this part as you do the one card spread reflections in Part 2.

Through this book and tarot, you will be able to see the answers that are already inside of you and take control of your life's story. Enjoy the process of learning more about tarot *and* yourself!

✴ Part 1 ✴

BEGINNING YOUR TAROT JOURNEY

The Universe is constantly sending messages—signs that you are on the right track, warnings about a challenge up ahead, advice on what step to take next... Some days, these signs are like flashing neon lights that you can't help but notice. Other days, they are subtle, even easy to miss in the chaos of everyday life.

How can you be sure you see these messages? And understand their meanings? With a one card tarot spread! But what exactly is tarot? And what is so special about one card spreads? In this part, you'll uncover the answers to these questions and more. Everything you need to begin divining the insights of tarot can be found here.

WHAT IS TAROT?

Before exploring the benefits of the one card spread, it's important to understand the basics of tarot, from what it is to how the cards in the deck are divided. Tarot is designed to solve the mysteries of our lives through depictions of everyday people in ordinary and extraordinary situations. It is the story of us as the heroes of our own epic life adventure! The cards we draw are trying to communicate something important about this story—the potential allies (and enemies) we may meet along the way, the strengths we have, the blind spots and shortcomings we may not acknowledge, and the situations we may find ourselves in or that have affected us in the past.

Brief Time Line of the Tarot

What we today consider to be tarot cards were likely first playing cards. It's believed that they were introduced to European ports and trading cities as an adaptation of Islamic Mamluk cards. Wealthy families in fifteenth-century Europe commissioned artists to customize these cards to portray their likenesses. It wasn't until the seventeenth century that history notes tarot cards being used as a divination system. In 1910, artist Pamela Colman Smith painted the seventy-eight cards in a collaboration with author A.E. Waite for his book *The Key to the Tarot*. Published by the Rider Company, the deck became the most popular tarot system today: the Rider–Waite–Smith deck.

Made up of seventy-eight cards, the tarot deck is divided into two sections: the Major Arcana and the Minor Arcana (*arcana* is Latin for "secrets"—fitting for such a mystical tool!). The Major Arcana is made up of twenty-two face cards that represent big-picture themes in your life—philosophical questions or subconscious forces you are facing. The Minor Arcana is made up of fifty-six cards divided into four suits: Wands, Swords, Cups, and Pentacles. While the Major Arcana is focused on larger life topics, the Minor Arcana is concerned with the everyday situations, challenges, and relationships you experience. In Part 3, you'll explore the Major and Minor Arcana in more detail.

◆ Trusting the Process

As you will discover in practicing one card spreads in Part 2, tarot can reveal the truth. It can show you answers that seem difficult to grasp at first but that are obvious in retrospect. It can even foretell events with literal accuracy!

It works because you did not randomly select that card in your hand. It's not a coincidence that the symbols on that card take on tangible form in your everyday life. Just like you reading this book right now is no coincidence. Tarot is not a game of chance. It's part of divine timing and your ability to see it, interpret it, and be an active part of how it manifests.

◆ Is Tarot Divination or Self-Actualization?

Whether it's noting how the movement of the planets correspond with specific situations or assigning definitions to the different images formed in tea leaves, people have always found meaning in the things that happen around them. Tarot is another pattern-based system that allows us to gain insight into the next likely sequence of events. Namely, it shows where your energy is flowing and how it is currently manifesting or likely will manifest.

As tarot readers, we are tapping in to the wisdom of the world—and the wisdom inside ourselves—when we consult the cards. This wisdom into the past, present, or future doesn't exactly speak in full sentences but rather prods us on an inner, intuitive level. We've always had the answers. It's just a matter of recognizing them. Tarot points you toward these answers, helping you figure out where to find them within by using certain symbols and pictures—shapes and colors as clues. Once you receive these clues, your intuition does the work of giving them significance, figuring out what they mean for your unique human experience.

That's the secret of tarot: It is both human and something that's trickier to pin down. Something less tangible—magical. And it can help you realize your dreams and purpose—and understand yourself with deeper gratitude!

TAROT AS A DAILY PRACTICE

When you use tarot as a daily practice, you are telling the Universe that you are aligning your everyday routine with your greater soul purpose. How? Simply by taking intentional time for yourself to prioritize the practice of this alignment. It becomes a meaningful self-care ritual.

And through this ritual, you are not only building your relationship with the Universe; you are also strengthening your confidence in yourself and your decision-making abilities. Now when a question comes up or you're faced with a series of choices, you'll be more prepared to navigate that scenario because you've built up your experiences on a smaller level by understanding the different cards. You'll be ready to apply everything you've learned more quickly and with more confidence.

As you build your relationship with tarot, you will also build trust: for yourself and your ability to regulate your emotions, to gain an objective viewpoint of difficulties you face, and to achieve your goals. But you'll also trust that there is something more to life than what your five senses can perceive. You'll trust that you have a personal coach in the spiritual plane who wants you to win. You'll see that the Universe has your back and knows how to communicate with you.

And it all starts with one card!

WHY YOU SHOULD READ ONE CARD SPREADS

Whether you're a seasoned tarot professional or just beginning your journey into reading the cards, one card spreads help deepen your spiritual practice because you're deepening your intuition, flexing your creative interpretation skills, and building your relationship with the powers that be—one card at a time. Now instead of looking up to the sky and asking for a sign, you can just look down at the one card you've drawn and find your sign right in your hand! The following are a few more reasons why you should read one card spreads.

◆ You Can Keep the Messages Concise

While using more cards in a tarot spread can add nuance and enhance the storytelling, the more cards you start pulling, the cloudier the main message can become. With one card spreads, you reflect on a few key symbols and themes. The one card method draws the specific energy of the moment you pull your card and directs you exactly to where you need to focus. Instead of multiple and potentially conflicting voices, you have one trusted guide—the card you pulled—to help you.

◆ There Is More Objectivity

Reading for yourself can feel hard. Staying objective about your personal situation is often challenging when you're so invested in what you think you want the outcome to be. One card spreads eliminate the doubt that comes from looking only at what you want to see (that burning desire in your own mind, the lens of your own restricted perspective). Instead, you'll face the answers provided by the themes and symbols of the card you draw. By understanding the ways each card can manifest, you'll get to know which cards offer a yes or a no answer, regardless of what you may *want* them to say.

◆ It Provides an Opportunity to Be Present

This method grounds you in the present moment. How? Drawing one card is an invitation to zoom in on what is happening right now, both within yourself and around you. Be intentional and focused as you carry out each step of the spread. Take note of any physical or emotional reactions to the card drawn. Have fun with the deck and your tarot journal. Leave regrets of the past and worries about the future behind (at least for now) as you build your present relationship with the cards, the Universe, and yourself.

With each card offering unique themes that will vary depending on the day, the question asked, and/or the situation you are facing, one card methods are a practice you will never get tired of, and they can only help you on your journey of practicing tarot and living a more spiritually grounded life.

KICK-START MANIFESTATION
——— ✦ ———

Setting an intention for your one card spread doesn't just focus your interpretation of the card drawn. It is also part of manifesting the things you want and letting the Universe (and yourself) know that you are committed to listening to whatever advice comes your way. You are ready to take action on your goals and nurture every part of your life, from your relationships with others to your career and finances. Your intention is the contract you are making with your higher self and the Universe to do just that. It is also the positive affirmation you put out in the world that attracts success along your journey.

TAROT MYTHS AND MISCONCEPTIONS

Before getting into the mechanics of doing a one card spread, there are a few misunderstandings about tarot that you will want to know. You may come across these during your own tarot journey, so it's important that the truth is clear. First, tarot readers are often stereotyped as grandiose fortune-tellers who make generic predictions—or dire ones. "You will meet a mysterious stranger." "You will receive a message." "You have a family curse that dooms your love life." "You will soon lose something you cherish." Either you walk away with some basic message that could apply to anyone, or you receive a vague dark warning. But the truth, as you have already read in the first pages of this book, is that tarot is designed to help you tap in to your own intuition and make more informed choices. Whether you are doing a reading alone or having one done for you, a good reader understands that they are simply a messenger relaying that inner wisdom—not masters of the future or fortune cookies come to life.

Now that you understand this, there are a few other misunderstandings to explore. The following are common myths linked to tarot.

MYTH 1 Tarot Is Only for Professional Psychics

This can be cleared up quickly: Tarot is for everyone because everyone *is* psychic. You don't need to self-identify as a psychic. The unseen forces all around you are just waiting for you to look for them. Practicing tarot doesn't mean you must read the cards professionally. Tarot can be something that you do just for you! Anyone who gatekeeps tarot by saying you shouldn't buy your own deck or telling you your interpretations are wrong is the one who's incorrect. Your experiences with tarot are unique to you, and so the relationship you create with the cards will also be unique.

MYTH 2 **Tarot Is Dangerous**

Drawing a tarot card, even a seemingly "scary" one, such as Death (which, you will learn in Part 3, is rarely as grim as it sounds), does not make anything happen. You are not inviting bad spirits, bad omens, or bad events when you draw a card. You are not to blame if the timing of an unfortunate situation coincides with having recently pulled a tarot card. You are not in control of the Universe! Fate and free will still apply. You are merely accessing information.

MYTH 3 **Your Deck Gets "Mad"**

You can ask the same question as many times as you'd like: Your tarot deck is not getting mad at you. It's not rolling its eyes at you, even if you are rolling your eyes at yourself (and if you are, tarot can help you practice more self-love and self-acceptance!). Tarot is like a gentle guide, a trusted mentor, a caring friend. And eventually, with practice, you'll see for yourself that it's part of your own higher self, speaking to you through the cards.

HOW TO CHOOSE YOUR DECK

Now that you know what's true—and not true—about tarot, it's time to choose the deck you'll use in Part 2. If you've ever shopped for clothes, you probably know that feeling when you've picked up an item you simply must have. It's almost electric—and the same goes with your tarot deck! Here's what to look for, whether shopping in person or online.

◆ Feel for an Instant Connection

Find a deck that has artwork and symbolism that speaks to you; there are no right or wrong choices here. You may prefer vibrant artwork with classical symbolism. Or artwork that is entirely animal-based. You could find yourself drawn to mystical decks featuring magical characters like unicorns, fairies, or vampires. Or decks featuring pop culture characters from a favorite TV show or movie. Other considerations will be size (maybe you want a pocket-sized version to take with you on the go or a large deck you can show off at home), shape (round or square cards might draw your eye), and the card stock and quality (your shuffling style can affect wear and tear).

◆ Choose a Tarot System

While this book works for whichever deck is used, a deck based on the classic Rider–Waite–Smith system is the most common one you will find on the market. Rider–Waite–Smith decks tend to include detailed artwork and symbolism that can be helpful as you grow your relationship with the cards. Other tarot systems, like the Thoth deck, incorporate more metaphysical symbolism and can be confusing to a beginner. But, as always, choose what resonates with you.

◆ Consider Your Needs

You may want to get different decks for different uses. For example, you might use a traditional Rider–Waite–Smith deck for daily one card pulls, but you may find that if love is a particular focus, you might prefer cards with romantic or sensual imagery, depicting scenes of lovers and couples and using symbols like hearts and roses. If you're using tarot to improve your relationship with finances, consider decks that have gold and silver trims, fonts, or imagery, or ones that use a lot of greens or earthy tones (colors of abundance).

HOW TO DO A ONE CARD SPREAD

———— ✦ ————

You've explored the basics of tarot and choosing a deck—now it's time for the fun part: taking out your tarot deck and digging into the intuitive wisdom within. The following are three easy steps for reading a one card tarot spread. Refer to these steps when pulling cards for the journal prompts in Part 2.

STEP 1 Set Your Intention

Preparing for a tarot reading can be as simple or as elaborate as you'd like, but you should always start with setting an intention. Before you begin, state what situation you'd like clarity on and make any desired appeals or direct addresses to the Universe. If you need inspiration, here is a simple intention you can say before asking an open-ended question:

> *Thank you* [Universe/the powers that be/etc.] *for assisting me today. I'd like to know what advice you have to share with me or what energy I'm being invited to focus on as I think about* [the issue you are facing].

An intention can also be centered around a promise (*I step toward the future with an optimistic mindset*) or a positive affirmation or mantra (*I am capable of anything I set my mind to*). In Part 2 of this book, you'll find a specific intention to use before each journal prompt in Chapters 1–6 to guide your focus on a certain topic or delve deeper into your subconscious. In Chapter 7, you will use the specific question you are asking to form your intention before shuffling and drawing an answer.

STEP 2 Shuffle, Shuffle, Shuffle

There are many ways to shuffle tarot decks, from splitting the deck or letting cards fall in short folds, to using "messy" shuffles or certain playing card shuffles. Do what feels right. As you shuffle, repeat your intention, picturing it in your mind. Shuffle for as long as feels right, but be sure that before you stop, you feel calm and relaxed instead of letting anxious thoughts influence your energy. Also notice if any cards fall out of the shuffle: This could be a signal for you to stop shuffling and use that card as your draw. Work with your intuition to see if this card feels like the answer. If no card pops out, continue shuffling until you feel called to stop.

STEP 3 Pull, Pause, and Ponder

Pull a card—from the top of the deck, the middle of the deck, or even from the bottom of the deck. You can also fan all the cards out and hover until you feel called to select one. Then flip the card over to see what wisdom and guidance is coming through for you. Note any initial gut reactions and spend a few moments reflecting on the card before you begin journaling.

What If the Card Is Upside Down?

Reversals (reversed cards, or cards that are drawn upside down) take on a special meaning; the message of the card should be given extra attention. The traditional meaning of the card is often flipped to mean the opposite, or the energy of the card might currently be blocked. A reversed card can be interpreted as taking on the card's "shadow" meaning (a meaning of repression, a personal weakness or shortcoming, etc.). In some instances, however, a reversal can mean that a period of hardship is ending but still present. If you're a beginner, it is recommended that you focus on the upright meanings of the cards. As you practice and hone your tarot reading skills, you can pay more attention to reversals if you choose.

An important note: Respect is essential. There is so much to uncover in just one card. Writing down your answers and reflections after selecting your card is crucial to this process. It shows that you are taking the answers and insights given with reverence. Pulling cards again and again because you don't like or don't immediately understand an initial answer may add to, not cut through, your confusion or dissatisfaction.

◆ Additional Ritual Elements

All you need for a one card spread is your deck, your intention, and your question, but as mentioned earlier in this section, you can get as elaborate with your ritual as you like. Pick a designated space you'll do your readings. Cover your desk or table with a tarot cloth (found in New Age stores or online). If you have any crystals, place them in your reading space (think rose quartz for love readings or clear quartz for general manifestation). Light a candle as you state your intention and stare into the flame as you repeat your intention out loud or in your head until it fully sinks in and other thoughts and feelings fade into the background. Burn a sweet-smelling incense to clear the energy of your reading space. The options for how you can create a ritual that resonates with you and what you are seeking from the cards are endless!

✳   ✳

What Does It Mean When Certain Cards Repeat?

Repeating cards (cards drawn more than once over a period of time) are a welcome sign during any part of your tarot journey. They remind you that your card pull is not random, even when it feels frustrating. A card may seem to follow you for days. It may appear no matter what kind of question you ask. It's a call for you to meditate on the card's energy. Journal about it, read about it, research it, and sit with it. What is your initial reaction to this card? What about its positive or negative manifestations do you or do you not want to acknowledge? You are being asked to pay attention to something. Are you implementing the card's message and working with it? When you have done so, the card will likely not repeat as often. And then when it does, you'll learn to greet it like a long-lost friend.

✳   ✳

Trust this process, especially in the beginning. As you get to more advanced or even intermediate stages, then you can begin to experiment with things like reversals, using decks with less imagery, or creating more elaborate pre-reading rituals.

TAKING THE NEXT STEP IN YOUR TAROT JOURNEY
——— ✦ ———

Now that you've explored the benefits of using tarot as a powerful tool for manifesting your goals and clueing in to the patterns and signs worth examining further, it's time for the fun part: drawing a card and digging into its special messages! Have your chosen deck(s) and a pen or pencil (a favorite marker works too!) handy as you unlock the insights this ancient tool has for you.

* Part 2 *

YOUR ONE CARD TAROT JOURNAL

Now that you have a better understanding of tarot and how one card spreads can benefit you, it's time to start your one card journal. The following pages are designed to help you use tarot to explore your relationships with yourself and others; to decide what life goals you want to achieve; to determine where to invest your time, money, and energy; to deepen your spirituality; to improve your emotional, mental, and physical health; and to get easy-to-understand insight on all of your burning questions.

Before starting your journal, be sure to take a look at the following information on best journaling practices and how to get the most out of each prompt. Your journey starts here.

HOW TO USE YOUR JOURNAL

Just as you get acquainted with your tarot deck, you should do the same with this journal. It is yours to write in, refer back to, and keep with you on a daily basis.

The journal prompts in each chapter are designed to help you hone your intuition, deepen your knowledge of tarot, and feel confident about making decisions that are aligned with your goals, values, and purpose.

You can use it every day or when you need clarity on a specific topic in life. You can also start at the beginning of the journal and work your way through, or flip around to what topics and/or prompts resonate on a given day. Regardless of how you use this journal, keep the following tips in mind as you work through each prompt:

1 **Hold space for your immediate reactions.** Drawing a card can be exhilarating, as the anticipation builds. You don't know what the advice or answer will be until you flip it over. In that in-between moment, you can gain a lot of insight into what you're hoping for, which is critical for building self-awareness.

2 **Jot down your reactions without self-judgment.** Did you feel excited or hopeful about the card's advice? Did you feel anxious or nervous? Did you feel disappointed? Notice any reactions, whether it was an emotional response or a physical one and then reflect without judgment on why you think that reaction occurred. This will be interesting information to look back on, to see how your reactions may change over time.

3 **Meditate on your card.** This can take as little as one minute. The time doesn't matter so much as the stillness you bring to your experience with journaling. Allow yourself to feel what you feel. And no matter how you feel, let the card's guidance and wisdom come through by letting go of expectations and control. Let its energy manifest as it is meant to in that moment.

◆ When to Use Your Journal

Consistency is key with developing any new skill. Learning tarot and deepening your intuition is no different, so it is recommended to use your one card journal every day, especially in the beginning of your journey. Not only will it help you grow your familiarity with your deck; you'll also learn how the cards' symbology is making itself apparent in your daily life.

Other factors to consider:

◆ **Are you a morning person?** If the answer is yes, make your journal part of your daily morning routine. It can take as little as five minutes to set your intention, shuffle your deck, pull your card, and reflect on your card of the day. It's a great way to get centered before you face the rest of your day.

◆ **Are you a night person?** If you get a creative burst in the later hours, work with that natural rhythm: Use your journal as part of your night-time bedtime routine. See if the card you draw appears in your dream or notice how its symbolism or artwork manifests the next day.

◆ **Do you have a specific question?** The prompts in this journal can help guide you at any time. From topics ranging from personal development and self-care, to love and relationships, to career and money, to spiritual development, you'll be inspired to gain insight into your most important relationships or your most pressing concerns. If you have a specific question in mind, use the open-ended journal prompts in Chapter 7 to record your question, the card's yes or no answer, and your personal reflections.

◆ What to Record about Your Reading

Every journal prompt will have sections to fill out basic information, like the date and time you pulled the card and what kind of card you pulled (Major or Minor Arcana, upright or reversed). Over time, you can begin to see what kind of patterns are emerging in your life, such as often pulling Cups cards in relation to love matters, or if Major Arcana cards appear whenever you ask a specific kind of question.

Each journal prompt starts with a positive affirmation for you to state first to help ground you in the moment of your tarot ritual and focus on high-vibrational energetic manifestation. Following the affirmation are the questions to consider as you write your reflection on the card drawn.

◆ How to Incorporate Your Reading Into Your Day

The fun of this journal is seeing how your chosen card manifests in your life. You are strongly encouraged to go about your day as you normally would. You may be tempted to put a lot of energy into actively scanning every moment for "a sign" from your card. That's perfectly understandable! But remember that the card's message will make itself known to you, regardless of how aware you are as you go through the activities of the day. You may find yourself seated in a certain position and realize you are replicating the Queen of Wands on her throne. Or you may look up and see a skull tattoo on a fellow passerby on a motorcycle in traffic—the Death card you pulled giving you a proverbial wink.

Ask Yourself These Questions

As you continue your tarot card journey, here are some helpful questions to keep in mind: Did the card's symbolism come through literally? For example, if there was a particular piece of artwork on the card, like a letter, a child, a rose, an animal, etc., perhaps it appeared to you in your day or as it related to your question. Was your experience more symbolic? Did one of the card's meanings or keywords (refer to the reference guide in Part 3) make its presence known to you to help provide clarity?

Come Back to the Prompts

Divine timing is just that; it works in its own time. Perhaps your situation is unfolding over the course of the day, week, or month. When you look back on an old journal prompt, you may find you see something you didn't before.

How have you changed? How has your relationship with the tarot deepened? How has your intuition strengthened? How have any of your previous assumptions about tarot or a specific card shifted? How have your perceptions of your situation changed?

CHOOSING YOUR TAROT CARD PERSONAL GUIDE

As you begin your one card journaling, ask the tarot which card can act as a personal guide for you through this journey. Think of this one card as your personal tarot mentor or companion—one you can go back to whenever you feel stuck or confused about a one card draw.

To start, shuffle the deck. Now draw your personal card and think of the spiritual medicine it can bring you as you deepen your relationship with not just the deck but also the practice of tarot as a whole.

Note: While it is encouraged that you try to resist the temptation to pull a clarifying card during your one card readings, especially if you're just beginning, it is okay to pick another card if you don't feel connected to the first personal guide card you chose. You want an instant spark—for this card to feel like a best friend, a trusted mentor, or a favored advisor. Pull a card until you land on the symbol, person, face, number, or keyword that feels right. When you have selected your guide (or, really, when your tarot personal guide has selected you!), journal about the experience in the following space.

And remember, everyone has multiple teachers in their lifetime. As you advance on your journey, you may decide it's time for a new personal guide. Thank your current guide, and then feel empowered to find a new teacher by starting the selection process all over again.

I am excited to embark on this journey to deepen my relationship with myself, with my intuition, and with the Universe through tarot.

Gently hold the deck in your hands and ask that the teacher that is meant to be your guide come forward as the next card you pull.

DATE .... TIME ....

TAROT GUIDE SELECTED ....

CARD TYPE
○ Major Arcana   ○ Minor Arcana

CARD POSITION
○ Upright   ○ Reversed

DECK USED ....

What drew me to this guide?
(Include any artwork, symbols, colors, prior associations, or any thoughts, feelings, or memories that stand out about this card.)

....

....

Based on either the traditional definition of this card or my own intuition, here are five to ten keywords I'll focus on with this card:

....

....

Intuitively, I believe my biggest challenge, as I open myself up to tarot and this journey, will be:

....

....

At the end of my journey, I want to feel:

....

....

....

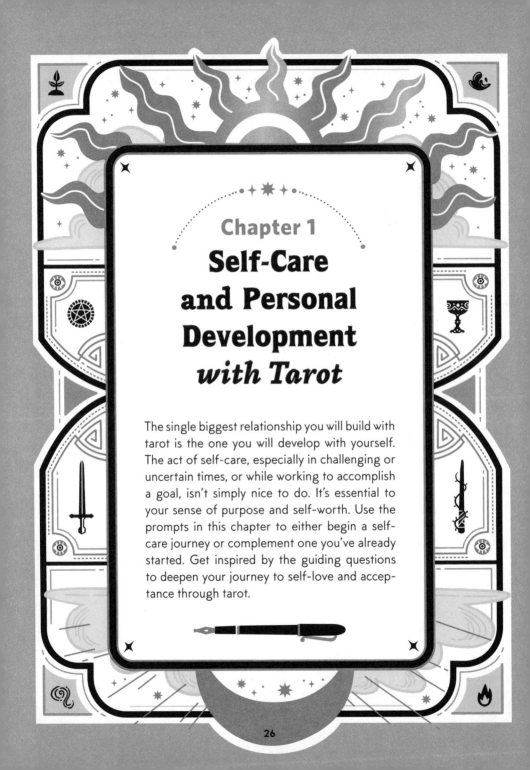

Chapter 1

Self-Care and Personal Development *with Tarot*

The single biggest relationship you will build with tarot is the one you will develop with yourself. The act of self-care, especially in challenging or uncertain times, or while working to accomplish a goal, isn't simply nice to do. It's essential to your sense of purpose and self-worth. Use the prompts in this chapter to either begin a self-care journey or complement one you've already started. Get inspired by the guiding questions to deepen your journey to self-love and acceptance through tarot.

JOURNAL PROMPT

I have many strengths and positive qualities that I admire in myself.

Based on the card you draw, what is a talent or skill you can appreciate about yourself and continue to hone right now?

DATE 6/18/2024   TIME 11:47

MY CARDS 1. 3 of swords 2. Knight of Cups 3. R. 9 of cups
4. 5 of wands 5. 10 of cups 6. THE SUN 7. 4 of cups 8. 1 of swords 9. 4 of pentacles
10. The honeydew

CARD TYPE
○ Major Arcana   ○ Minor Arcana

CARD POSITION
○ Upright   ○ Reversed

What feelings came up when I pulled this card?

I was feeling how I just wanted to know what I got going on in my life Right now and what it was going to Bring the

What elements of the card's meaning resonate with me and this prompt?

The Sun.

Which deck did I use? What artwork spoke to me?

I used my usual Deck. And it was on point

My prompt response and reflections:

JOURNAL PROMPT

Although I strive to do my best in every situation,
I acknowledge and accept where I have let myself down.

Forgiveness, especially of yourself, is an important step
in healing. What is the card you draw saying that you can
release in order to forgive yourself for a past mistake?

DATE 6/20/24   TIME

MY CARD 4 wands / 2 pentacals / pace wands

CARD TYPE
O Major Arcana   ⊗ Minor Arcana

CARD POSITION
⊗ Upright   O Reversed

What feelings came up when I pulled this card?

I have been completly stressed about moving. And
now Im going to manage.

What elements of the card's meaning resonate with me and this prompt?

Each card Resonated with me. The Honeymoon phase.
Because of the New thing I have with Someone, But
eh.

Which deck did I use? What artwork spoke to me?

2 of penticals Spoke to me. I have to move and Im
super stressed about money. I need more guidence

My prompt response and reflections:

This pull was exactly what I got going
on right Now Im In the middle of Some Big
decesions about moving.

JOURNAL PROMPT

I seek out spontaneity and adventure to cultivate more joy in my life.

Choose a card that depicts an area of life that you can develop
or explore that you may not have previously considered.

DATE .... TIME ....

MY CARD ....

CARD TYPE
○ Major Arcana   ○ Minor Arcana

CARD POSITION
○ Upright   ○ Reversed

What feelings came up when I pulled this card?

....

....

What elements of the card's meaning resonate with me and this prompt?

....

....

Which deck did I use? What artwork spoke to me?

....

....

My prompt response and reflections:

....

....

....

....

....

....

....

....

JOURNAL PROMPT

I am kind to my body, I am kind to my mind, I am kind to myself.

When a moment of self-criticism or self-judgment arises, draw a tarot card and reflect on its advice for how to practice more kindness and self-compassion for every aspect of yourself.

DATE .... TIME ....

MY CARD ....

CARD TYPE
○ Major Arcana   ○ Minor Arcana

CARD POSITION
○ Upright   ○ Reversed

What feelings came up when I pulled this card?

....
....

What elements of the card's meaning resonate with me and this prompt?

....
....

Which deck did I use? What artwork spoke to me?

....
....

My prompt response and reflections:

....
....
....
....
....
....
....

While it is important for others to like me, I know it is essential that I like me.

Seeking external validation is normal, but it can also point to an area about which you feel insecure. What can the tarot card you draw help you understand about that underlying feeling so you can begin to self-validate?

DATE .... TIME ....

MY CARD ....

CARD TYPE | CARD POSITION
O Major Arcana O Minor Arcana | O Upright O Reversed

What feelings came up when I pulled this card?

....

....

What elements of the card's meaning resonate with me and this prompt?

....

....

Which deck did I use? What artwork spoke to me?

....

....

My prompt response and reflections:

....

....

....

....

....

....

....

....

JOURNAL PROMPT

Change is constant. I understand it is my soul contract with the Universe.

Feeling overwhelmed or anxious about change happens to everyone. Draw a card for insight into what you can expect to feel during a change that has recently occurred.

DATE .... TIME ....

MY CARD ....

CARD TYPE
○ Major Arcana ○ Minor Arcana

CARD POSITION
○ Upright ○ Reversed

What feelings came up when I pulled this card?

....
....

What elements of the card's meaning resonate with me and this prompt?

....
....

Which deck did I use? What artwork spoke to me?

....
....

My prompt response and reflections:

....
....
....
....
....
....
....

JOURNAL PROMPT

I enjoy my daydreams, as they are a safe and fun space for me to be myself.

Daydreaming and free association can help unpack hidden desires or motivations in your subconscious. Draw a card to help guide you during your next daydream, mindful meditation, or free association writing exercise. What does this card say about what you might want more of from your daily life or what you feel you may be missing?

DATE .... TIME ....

MY CARD ....

CARD TYPE
○ Major Arcana   ○ Minor Arcana

CARD POSITION
○ Upright   ○ Reversed

What feelings came up when I pulled this card?

....

....

What elements of the card's meaning resonate with me and this prompt?

....

....

Which deck did I use? What artwork spoke to me?

....

....

My prompt response and reflections:

....

....

....

....

....

....

....

JOURNAL PROMPT

*Time is a gift and that is why I prioritize what is
most important and valuable to me.*

As you juggle multiple priorities and competing deadlines in
your routine, you may struggle with prioritization. Draw a card
for insight into what needs should take top priority in your day
so you can release any obligations that don't serve you.

DATE ....   TIME ....

MY CARD ....

CARD TYPE   CARD POSITION
○ Major Arcana   ○ Minor Arcana   ○ Upright   ○ Reversed

What feelings came up when I pulled this card?

....

....

What elements of the card's meaning resonate with me and this prompt?

....

....

Which deck did I use? What artwork spoke to me?

....

....

My prompt response and reflections:

....

....

....

....

....

....

+ ———— **JOURNAL PROMPT** ———— +

What I am most proud of is the time I [insert moment here].

Reflect on a time in your life you were most proud of yourself. Then draw a card to help you gain a deeper understanding of how you saw yourself during that time and what you can do to feel like that again.

DATE .... TIME ....

MY CARD ....

CARD TYPE

○ Major Arcana ○ Minor Arcana

CARD POSITION

○ Upright ○ Reversed

What feelings came up when I pulled this card?

....

....

What elements of the card's meaning resonate with me and this prompt?

....

....

Which deck did I use? What artwork spoke to me?

....

....

My prompt response and reflections:

....

....

....

....

....

....

....

....

+ ——— **JOURNAL PROMPT** ——— +

I am my own best friend and personal cheerleader.

If you have an inner critic inside your head, it can block you from accomplishing your goals. Use one of the positive keywords (see Part 3) of the card you draw to help reframe what your critic is saying and release any blocks to your success.

DATE .... TIME ....

MY CARD ....

CARD TYPE
O Major Arcana   O Minor Arcana

CARD POSITION
O Upright   O Reversed

What feelings came up when I pulled this card?

....
....

What elements of the card's meaning resonate with me and this prompt?

....
....

Which deck did I use? What artwork spoke to me?

....
....

My prompt response and reflections:

....
....
....
....
....
....

JOURNAL PROMPT

I am open to reparenting my inner child.

Draw a card and use its keywords or imagined persona to write a short letter to your inner child from a time you wished you had more comforting words or wise perspective to help you cope or understand a challenging time. What kindness would this card offer to your inner child?

DATE .... TIME ....

MY CARD ....

CARD TYPE
O Major Arcana   O Minor Arcana

CARD POSITION
O Upright   O Reversed

What feelings came up when I pulled this card?

....

....

What elements of the card's meaning resonate with me and this prompt?

....

....

Which deck did I use? What artwork spoke to me?

....

....

My prompt response and reflections:

....

....

....

....

....

....

....

JOURNAL PROMPT

I am kind to myself about what I see in myself and what I don't.

What talent or trait, hidden or overt, is the card you draw telling you that you have but don't fully understand or appreciate?

DATE .... TIME ....

MY CARD ....

CARD TYPE
○ Major Arcana ○ Minor Arcana

CARD POSITION
○ Upright ○ Reversed

What feelings came up when I pulled this card?

What elements of the card's meaning resonate with me and this prompt?

Which deck did I use? What artwork spoke to me?

My prompt response and reflections:

JOURNAL PROMPT

I am always striving to better myself.

The Universe wants to see you succeed. Look to the card you draw as a special message of what your highest self and the powers that be want you to know about yourself in this moment and ways you can improve.

DATE .... TIME ....

MY CARD ....

CARD TYPE
○ Major Arcana ○ Minor Arcana

CARD POSITION
○ Upright ○ Reversed

What feelings came up when I pulled this card?

....
....

What elements of the card's meaning resonate with me and this prompt?

....
....

Which deck did I use? What artwork spoke to me?

....
....

My prompt response and reflections:

....
....
....
....
....
....
....
....

JOURNAL PROMPT

I welcome change by facing it head on.

Change can be hard, especially as it can make you feel out of control. As you reflect on what you need or do to feel in control, draw a tarot card to help you understand the underlying feeling(s) you associate with feeling out of control. Why do you associate it with these feelings?

DATE .... TIME ....

MY CARD ....

CARD TYPE
○ Major Arcana ○ Minor Arcana

CARD POSITION
○ Upright ○ Reversed

What feelings came up when I pulled this card?

....

....

What elements of the card's meaning resonate with me and this prompt?

....

....

Which deck did I use? What artwork spoke to me?

....

....

My prompt response and reflections:

....

....

....

....

....

....

....

+ ———————— **JOURNAL PROMPT** ———————— +

While I value my opinions, they do not define me.
I allow myself to grow, evolve, and change.

Think of a topic that prompts strong feelings or reactions in you.
What does the card you draw say about those feelings/reactions
(where they come from, why they are so strong)? Consider what
advice it is sharing about how you can constructively communicate
your thoughts on that topic without alienating others.

DATE .... TIME ....

MY CARD ....

CARD TYPE   CARD POSITION
○ Major Arcana   ○ Minor Arcana   ○ Upright   ○ Reversed

What feelings came up when I pulled this card?

....
....

What elements of the card's meaning resonate with me and this prompt?

....
....

Which deck did I use? What artwork spoke to me?

....
....

My prompt response and reflections:

....
....
....
....
....
....

+ —————— **JOURNAL PROMPT** —————— +

*I accept with grace that certain events have led to
feelings of regret or disappointment.*

Think about an event that didn't turn out the way you wanted
or expected. What does the card you draw say about why
that event happened the way it did and how you can release
any negative associations you have with this outcome?

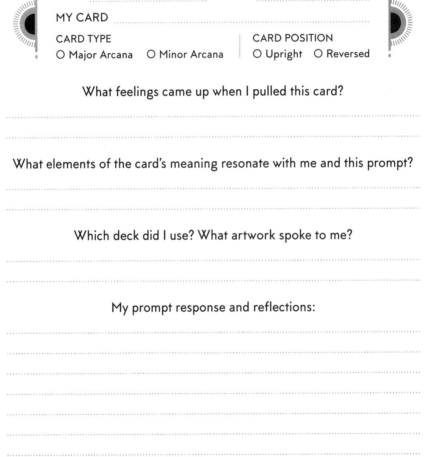

DATE .... TIME ....

MY CARD ....

CARD TYPE
○ Major Arcana   ○ Minor Arcana

CARD POSITION
○ Upright   ○ Reversed

What feelings came up when I pulled this card?

....
....

What elements of the card's meaning resonate with me and this prompt?

....
....

Which deck did I use? What artwork spoke to me?

....
....

My prompt response and reflections:

....
....
....
....
....
....

I am an adventurous person in body and spirit.

Draw a card to get inspired about a new opportunity, new hobby, or new adventure you can explore in your life. Use the card's keywords or artwork as a guide: Is there a symbol about writing? Does the card indicate travel or vacation? What about the outdoors?

DATE .... TIME ....

MY CARD ....

CARD TYPE
O Major Arcana   O Minor Arcana

CARD POSITION
O Upright   O Reversed

What feelings came up when I pulled this card?

....

....

What elements of the card's meaning resonate with me and this prompt?

....

....

Which deck did I use? What artwork spoke to me?

....

....

My prompt response and reflections:

....

....

....

....

....

....

JOURNAL PROMPT

I am a consistent work in progress.

Focusing on your perceived weaknesses can create limiting thought patterns and behaviors. Draw a tarot card to see how the card's positive attributes can help you redefine something you perceive as a weakness to see how it is actually one of your strengths.

DATE .... TIME ....

MY CARD ....

CARD TYPE
○ Major Arcana ○ Minor Arcana

CARD POSITION
○ Upright ○ Reversed

What feelings came up when I pulled this card?

....
....

What elements of the card's meaning resonate with me and this prompt?

....
....

Which deck did I use? What artwork spoke to me?

....
....

My prompt response and reflections:

....
....
....
....
....
....
....

JOURNAL PROMPT

I have goals I want to achieve like [insert one personal goal here].

Think about something you want to accomplish—get married, write a book, finish a marathon, etc. What does the card you draw say about why this goal feels so important to you and your life's purpose?

DATE .... TIME ....

MY CARD ....

CARD TYPE
○ Major Arcana ○ Minor Arcana

CARD POSITION
○ Upright ○ Reversed

What feelings came up when I pulled this card?

....
....

What elements of the card's meaning resonate with me and this prompt?

....
....

Which deck did I use? What artwork spoke to me?

....
....

My prompt response and reflections:

....
....
....
....
....
....
....

+ ——— **JOURNAL PROMPT** ——— +

I accept my emotions, even the ones that make me feel uncomfortable.

Feeling emotions, even the uncomfortable ones, is part of the human experience. What feeling is the card you draw telling you to prioritize experiencing right now as a part of self-care and self-healing?

DATE .... TIME ....

MY CARD ....

CARD TYPE
O Major Arcana   O Minor Arcana

CARD POSITION
O Upright   O Reversed

What feelings came up when I pulled this card?

....
....

What elements of the card's meaning resonate with me and this prompt?

....
....

Which deck did I use? What artwork spoke to me?

....
....

My prompt response and reflections:

....
....
....
....
....
....
....
....

+ ———— **JOURNAL PROMPT** ———— +

I acknowledge what I am responsible for—and what I cannot control.

Healthy boundaries are an essential part of self-care. In what parts of your life and relationships is the card you draw telling you that you may need to strengthen your boundaries with others, situations, places, etc., in order to protect your well-being? Why are the current boundaries not enough?

DATE .... TIME ....

MY CARD ....

CARD TYPE
O Major Arcana   O Minor Arcana

CARD POSITION
O Upright   O Reversed

What feelings came up when I pulled this card?

....

....

What elements of the card's meaning resonate with me and this prompt?

....

....

Which deck did I use? What artwork spoke to me?

....

....

My prompt response and reflections:

....

....

....

....

....

....

....

+———— **JOURNAL PROMPT** ————+

Having fun is crucial to my mental, physical, and emotional well-being.

Feeling stuck in a rut can be common. Draw a tarot card and use the symbols, artwork, or keywords of the card to get inspired to do one fun, new activity. Does the card show someone outside or in a scene of nature? Is water symbolism inspiring any ideas? Is there a person depicted on the tarot card that makes you want to call someone you know?

DATE .... TIME ....

MY CARD ....

CARD TYPE   CARD POSITION
○ Major Arcana   ○ Minor Arcana   ○ Upright   ○ Reversed

What feelings came up when I pulled this card?

What elements of the card's meaning resonate with me and this prompt?

Which deck did I use? What artwork spoke to me?

My prompt response and reflections:

JOURNAL PROMPT

I only want to spend time doing activities that fill me with joy.

At some points in time, certain projects could be draining you, but letting go can be difficult. What is that thing that is draining you of your energy? What does the card you draw show you about how you can release this with kindness to yourself?

DATE .... TIME ....

MY CARD ....

CARD TYPE
○ Major Arcana   ○ Minor Arcana

CARD POSITION
○ Upright   ○ Reversed

What feelings came up when I pulled this card?

....
....

What elements of the card's meaning resonate with me and this prompt?

....
....

Which deck did I use? What artwork spoke to me?

....
....

My prompt response and reflections:

....
....
....
....
....
....
....

JOURNAL PROMPT

I desire inner and outer peace.

Finding a place to call home, literally or figuratively, is essential to feeling safe. What feels like home to you? What can the card you draw show you about what you need in order to feel a sense of security and comfort?

DATE .... TIME ....

MY CARD ....

CARD TYPE
O Major Arcana   O Minor Arcana

CARD POSITION
O Upright   O Reversed

What feelings came up when I pulled this card?

....
....

What elements of the card's meaning resonate with me and this prompt?

....
....

Which deck did I use? What artwork spoke to me?

....
....

My prompt response and reflections:

....
....
....
....
....
....
....

JOURNAL PROMPT

I am excited about my future.

Write a letter to your future self from the perspective of the tarot card you pull. Personify that card, either based on the character or archetype of that card or using some of the keywords in Part 3.

DATE .... TIME ....

MY CARD ....

CARD TYPE
○ Major Arcana ○ Minor Arcana

CARD POSITION
○ Upright ○ Reversed

What feelings came up when I pulled this card?

....

....

What elements of the card's meaning resonate with me and this prompt?

....

....

Which deck did I use? What artwork spoke to me?

....

....

My prompt response and reflections:

....

....

....

....

....

....

....

Chapter 2
Love and Relationships *with Tarot*

People can spend a lot of time thinking, fantasizing, talking, or writing about love, chasing after it, and even ignoring or denying it. But love isn't something you have to search for. It is an infinite source that already exists inside of you. Sometimes you may just need help accessing it. And that is where your relationships with others are essential. Friends, family, partners, and other people you hold dear allow you to both give and receive love, and deepen your understanding of it. The following journal prompts will help you access this wellspring and claim what the tarot can guide you to achieve: feeling love for yourself and others.

─────── **JOURNAL PROMPT** ───────

I love the qualities that my partner (or a person I admire) has in abundance.

Traits you admire in other people can help you better understand what you seek to improve or accept about yourself. Meditate on a person you admire: a partner, a loved one, even a favorite celebrity. Then draw a card to understand where and how to take action in your life to cultivate this quality in yourself.

DATE .... TIME ....

MY CARD ....

CARD TYPE
○ Major Arcana   ○ Minor Arcana

CARD POSITION
○ Upright   ○ Reversed

What feelings came up when I pulled this card?

....

....

What elements of the card's meaning resonate with me and this prompt?

....

....

Which deck did I use? What artwork spoke to me?

....

....

My prompt response and reflections:

....

....

....

....

....

....

....

+ ——— **JOURNAL PROMPT** ——— +

I desire a loving and committed relationship.

According to the card you draw, what is currently blocking you from accepting and experiencing the love you seek?

DATE .... TIME ....

MY CARD ....

CARD TYPE
○ Major Arcana   ○ Minor Arcana

CARD POSITION
○ Upright   ○ Reversed

What feelings came up when I pulled this card?

....

....

What elements of the card's meaning resonate with me and this prompt?

....

....

Which deck did I use? What artwork spoke to me?

....

....

My prompt response and reflections:

....

....

....

....

....

....

....

....

+ ———— **JOURNAL PROMPT** ———— +

I am surrounded by people who see the best in me.

Think about the last compliment you received. How did it make you feel? Incorporate the keywords of the card you draw (see Part 3) into your journal entry about how this experience went for you.

DATE .... TIME ....

MY CARD ....

CARD TYPE
O Major Arcana O Minor Arcana

CARD POSITION
O Upright O Reversed

What feelings came up when I pulled this card?

....
....

What elements of the card's meaning resonate with me and this prompt?

....
....

Which deck did I use? What artwork spoke to me?

....
....

My prompt response and reflections:

....
....
....
....
....
....
....
....

+——————— **JOURNAL PROMPT** ———————+

I seek relationships where I feel seen without judgment.

Think about a belief or situation where you feel unfairly criticized
or misunderstood. What is something you wish others knew about
you? Draw a card to guide your reflection on this and consider
how you can better communicate this to others in your life.

DATE .... TIME ....

MY CARD ....

CARD TYPE   CARD POSITION
○ Major Arcana ○ Minor Arcana   ○ Upright ○ Reversed

What feelings came up when I pulled this card?

....

....

What elements of the card's meaning resonate with me and this prompt?

....

....

Which deck did I use? What artwork spoke to me?

....

....

My prompt response and reflections:

....

....

....

....

....

....

+ ——— JOURNAL PROMPT ——— +

I can still love other people even when they upset or disappointment me.

If someone you care about disappoints you, it doesn't mean that they are a bad person or that they don't care about you. But advocating for yourself is important. You may feel the need to express your disappointment in order to reach a compromise. Use one (or more) of the keywords associated with the card you draw to help you reflect on and then express to someone how their disappointing action(s) made you feel.

DATE ....   TIME ....

MY CARD ....

CARD TYPE   CARD POSITION
○ Major Arcana   ○ Minor Arcana   ○ Upright   ○ Reversed

What feelings came up when I pulled this card?

....

....

What elements of the card's meaning resonate with me and this prompt?

....

....

Which deck did I use? What artwork spoke to me?

....

....

My prompt response and reflections:

....

....

....

....

....

....

JOURNAL PROMPT

I attract love to me.

Use the card you draw to understand the qualities you most seek and desire in an ideal partner. Write a love letter to that person.

DATE .... TIME ....

MY CARD ....

CARD TYPE
○ Major Arcana ○ Minor Arcana

CARD POSITION
○ Upright ○ Reversed

What feelings came up when I pulled this card?

....
....

What elements of the card's meaning resonate with me and this prompt?

....
....

Which deck did I use? What artwork spoke to me?

....
....

My prompt response and reflections:

....
....
....
....
....
....
....
....

✦ ──────── **JOURNAL PROMPT** ──────── ✦

I am worthy of the love I seek.

If you are seeking a new love, now is the time to ask the Universe for guidance. Draw a card to learn what signs or symbols to look for to confirm you're on the right path to finding the love you seek. Are you being inspired to go out more? To join a dating website?

DATE .... TIME ....

MY CARD ....

CARD TYPE
○ Major Arcana   ○ Minor Arcana

CARD POSITION
○ Upright   ○ Reversed

What feelings came up when I pulled this card?

....
....

What elements of the card's meaning resonate with me and this prompt?

....
....

Which deck did I use? What artwork spoke to me?

....
....

My prompt response and reflections:

....
....
....
....
....
....
....

✦——————— **JOURNAL PROMPT** ———————✦

I am a loving and kind energetic soul and I attract like-minded people to me.

According to the card you draw, what positive qualities does
your partner most admire in you or you in them?

DATE .... TIME ....

MY CARD ....

CARD TYPE
○ Major Arcana   ○ Minor Arcana

CARD POSITION
○ Upright   ○ Reversed

What feelings came up when I pulled this card?

....
....

What elements of the card's meaning resonate with me and this prompt?

....
....

Which deck did I use? What artwork spoke to me?

....
....

My prompt response and reflections:

....
....
....
....
....
....
....
....
....
....

I attract a love that matches my daydreams.

If you had everything you wanted in love, how would that feel? Think about the daydreams you have about love and how you can make them a reality. Draw a card to understand what you need to know about your expectations and desires in a love relationship.

DATE .... TIME ....

MY CARD ....

CARD TYPE
O Major Arcana   O Minor Arcana

CARD POSITION
O Upright   O Reversed

What feelings came up when I pulled this card?

....
....

What elements of the card's meaning resonate with me and this prompt?

....
....

Which deck did I use? What artwork spoke to me?

....
....

My prompt response and reflections:

....
....
....
....
....
....
....

+ ──────── **JOURNAL PROMPT** ──────── +

I acknowledge that sometimes partnerships can be challenging.

Working through disagreements with your partner is character building for both of you. But it can also take a lot of effort. What does the card you draw show you about this experience and what the commitment to your partner means to you?

DATE .... TIME ....

MY CARD ....

CARD TYPE | CARD POSITION
○ Major Arcana   ○ Minor Arcana | ○ Upright   ○ Reversed

What feelings came up when I pulled this card?

....
....

What elements of the card's meaning resonate with me and this prompt?

....
....

Which deck did I use? What artwork spoke to me?

....
....

My prompt response and reflections:

....
....
....
....
....
....

♦ ─── JOURNAL PROMPT ─── ♦

I welcome love, especially unconditional love, in all the ways it comes to me.

Think about your concept of unconditional love. Do you take any of the love you receive for granted? Based on the card you draw, how can you show more gratitude to a person who provides unconditional love to you?

DATE .... TIME ....

MY CARD ....

CARD TYPE
O Major Arcana   O Minor Arcana

CARD POSITION
O Upright   O Reversed

What feelings came up when I pulled this card?

....

....

What elements of the card's meaning resonate with me and this prompt?

....

....

Which deck did I use? What artwork spoke to me?

....

....

My prompt response and reflections:

....

....

....

....

....

....

....

....

✦ ─── **JOURNAL PROMPT** ─── ✦

I am an attractive person who magnetizes love.

What is a self-limiting thought or belief you have about yourself? Use the card's more challenging qualities to help answer this question. How can you release that thought/belief in order to attract love and tenderness? Use the card's more positive qualities to help you reframe this thought or belief.

DATE .... TIME ....

MY CARD ....

CARD TYPE
○ Major Arcana   ○ Minor Arcana

CARD POSITION
○ Upright   ○ Reversed

What feelings came up when I pulled this card?

....

....

What elements of the card's meaning resonate with me and this prompt?

....

....

Which deck did I use? What artwork spoke to me?

....

....

My prompt response and reflections:

....

....

....

....

....

....

....

JOURNAL PROMPT

I release anger, regret, or resentment toward myself or others.

Think about a grudge you are holding and why. Then use the card you draw to help show you how to release this grudge so you no longer carry this weight and negativity. Is it through a physical activity like a conversation? Writing? Or is the tarot calling for you to process this emotionally, like through love, forgiveness, or acceptance?

DATE .... TIME ....

MY CARD ....

CARD TYPE
O Major Arcana   O Minor Arcana

CARD POSITION
O Upright   O Reversed

What feelings came up when I pulled this card?

....
....

What elements of the card's meaning resonate with me and this prompt?

....
....

Which deck did I use? What artwork spoke to me?

....
....

My prompt response and reflections:

....
....
....
....
....
....
....

JOURNAL PROMPT

I am comfortable breaking out of comfort zones in relationships.

Whether you're in one or longing to be in one, relationships take work. What is something you can be open to experiencing in love that you haven't considered before? Based on the card you draw, how can you keep the spark going or maintain a relationship you value?

DATE .... TIME ....

MY CARD ....

CARD TYPE
○ Major Arcana   ○ Minor Arcana

CARD POSITION
○ Upright   ○ Reversed

What feelings came up when I pulled this card?

....
....

What elements of the card's meaning resonate with me and this prompt?

....
....

Which deck did I use? What artwork spoke to me?

....
....

My prompt response and reflections:

....
....
....
....
....
....
....

JOURNAL PROMPT

I give from the heart.

Whether it's a birthday, anniversary, holiday, or just because, when you give a heartfelt gift to someone you love, it's a message. Pull a card and use its themes to reflect on a gift you can give someone from your heart. Is it time? A feeling? Or is there a symbol or something in the artwork that inspires you in giving a certain gift?

DATE .... TIME ....

MY CARD ....

CARD TYPE
O Major Arcana   O Minor Arcana

CARD POSITION
O Upright   O Reversed

What feelings came up when I pulled this card?

....

....

What elements of the card's meaning resonate with me and this prompt?

....

....

Which deck did I use? What artwork spoke to me?

....

....

My prompt response and reflections:

....

....

....

....

....

....

JOURNAL PROMPT

I love myself wholly and completely.

Write yourself a love letter from the perspective of the card you choose, using the card's archetype or keywords from Part 3. Feel free to go over the top describing how madly, totally in love this card is with you. Allow yourself to see yourself in someone else's loving gaze.

DATE .... TIME ....

MY CARD ....

CARD TYPE
○ Major Arcana   ○ Minor Arcana

CARD POSITION
○ Upright   ○ Reversed

What feelings came up when I pulled this card?

....

....

What elements of the card's meaning resonate with me and this prompt?

....

....

Which deck did I use? What artwork spoke to me?

....

....

My prompt response and reflections:

....

....

....

....

....

....

....

+ ——— **JOURNAL PROMPT** ——— +

*I acknowledge that love can change over time, even if that
means that relationships have to change or end as well.*

Reflect on a previous heartbreak or romantic situation that ended
in a way you didn't want. Then draw a card to help deepen your
understanding of the lesson(s) you learned from this experience—
specifically about self-value and honoring your feelings.

DATE .... TIME ....

MY CARD ....

CARD TYPE   CARD POSITION
○ Major Arcana   ○ Minor Arcana   ○ Upright   ○ Reversed

What feelings came up when I pulled this card?

....

....

What elements of the card's meaning resonate with me and this prompt?

....

....

Which deck did I use? What artwork spoke to me?

....

....

My prompt response and reflections:

....

....

....

....

....

....

JOURNAL PROMPT

I am open to receiving loving care and support.

Everyone needs help sometimes. Feeling safe enough to ask for it is one of the best parts of having a dedicated partner. What can the card you draw show you about a time you felt loved, supported, and respected by your partner—or a time you didn't?

DATE .... TIME ....

MY CARD ....

CARD TYPE | CARD POSITION
O Major Arcana   O Minor Arcana | O Upright   O Reversed

What feelings came up when I pulled this card?

....
....

What elements of the card's meaning resonate with me and this prompt?

....
....

Which deck did I use? What artwork spoke to me?

....
....

My prompt response and reflections:

....
....
....
....
....
....
....

I accept that I do not have to be perfect to receive love.

No one is perfect—but everyone deserves love anyway. Think of
a time when you felt loved without condition or judgment. What
might the card you draw show you about that experience?

DATE .... TIME ....

MY CARD ....

CARD TYPE | CARD POSITION
○ Major Arcana ○ Minor Arcana | ○ Upright ○ Reversed

What feelings came up when I pulled this card?

....

....

What elements of the card's meaning resonate with me and this prompt?

....

....

Which deck did I use? What artwork spoke to me?

....

....

My prompt response and reflections:

....

....

....

....

....

....

....

....

+ ———— **JOURNAL PROMPT** ———— +

I love love, in all its forms and iterations.

Love has many definitions. It means many different things to many different people. What does it mean to you? Draw a card to help guide your reflection.

DATE .... TIME ....

MY CARD ....

CARD TYPE
○ Major Arcana   ○ Minor Arcana

CARD POSITION
○ Upright   ○ Reversed

What feelings came up when I pulled this card?

....

....

What elements of the card's meaning resonate with me and this prompt?

....

....

Which deck did I use? What artwork spoke to me?

....

....

My prompt response and reflections:

....

....

....

....

....

....

....

....

--- + **JOURNAL PROMPT** + ---

My first love still leaves a heartfelt impression on me.

Think about your first experience of love. It could be a first partner, a first crush, or a celebrity you admired. Gather insight from the card you pull regarding what impression this first love left on you and what it says about how you define romance.

DATE .... TIME ....

MY CARD ....

CARD TYPE
○ Major Arcana ○ Minor Arcana

CARD POSITION
○ Upright ○ Reversed

What feelings came up when I pulled this card?

....

....

What elements of the card's meaning resonate with me and this prompt?

....

....

Which deck did I use? What artwork spoke to me?

....

....

My prompt response and reflections:

....

....

....

....

....

....

....

+ ———— **JOURNAL PROMPT** ———— +

I am willing to put in effort to make my important relationships work.

Think of the most important relationships currently in your life. Draw a card while reflecting on a consistent theme throughout these dynamics. Using the insights of the card, determine what that theme is and what it can show you about the effort you may need to put in or adjust to maintain those relationships.

DATE .... TIME ....

MY CARD ....

CARD TYPE   CARD POSITION
○ Major Arcana   ○ Minor Arcana   ○ Upright   ○ Reversed

What feelings came up when I pulled this card?

....

....

What elements of the card's meaning resonate with me and this prompt?

....

....

Which deck did I use? What artwork spoke to me?

....

....

My prompt response and reflections:

....

....

....

....

....

....

....

JOURNAL PROMPT

I want relationships that feel solid and consistent.
I release those that leave me confused.

There are certain relationships that leave you feeling unsure or confused about where you stand with another person. If mixed signals are present, what can the card you draw tell you about what they mean?

DATE .... TIME ....

MY CARD ....

CARD TYPE
○ Major Arcana ○ Minor Arcana

CARD POSITION
○ Upright ○ Reversed

What feelings came up when I pulled this card?

....

....

What elements of the card's meaning resonate with me and this prompt?

....

....

Which deck did I use? What artwork spoke to me?

....

....

My prompt response and reflections:

....

....

....

....

....

....

+ ──────── **JOURNAL PROMPT** ──────── +

I communicate authentically and honestly.

Communication in a relationship is critical to its long-term success. Think about a relationship in which you hold back from saying exactly what you mean or how you feel. Before drawing a card, ask the deck to show you what open communication with this person would look like. Reflect on the answer.

DATE .... TIME ....

MY CARD ....

CARD TYPE
○ Major Arcana ○ Minor Arcana

CARD POSITION
○ Upright ○ Reversed

What feelings came up when I pulled this card?

....

....

What elements of the card's meaning resonate with me and this prompt?

....

....

Which deck did I use? What artwork spoke to me?

....

....

My prompt response and reflections:

....

....

....

....

....

....

+ ─────── **JOURNAL PROMPT** ─────── +

*Spending time with someone is the greatest gift anyone
can give me or that I can give to anyone.*

Think about planning a date with your partner. Where will you go? What
will you do? What is the dress code? Use the symbols, keywords, and/
or artwork of the card you draw to brainstorm a new date idea.

DATE .... TIME ....

MY CARD ....

CARD TYPE   CARD POSITION
○ Major Arcana   ○ Minor Arcana   ○ Upright   ○ Reversed

What feelings came up when I pulled this card?

....
....

What elements of the card's meaning resonate with me and this prompt?

....
....

Which deck did I use? What artwork spoke to me?

....
....

My prompt response and reflections:

....
....
....
....
....
....
....

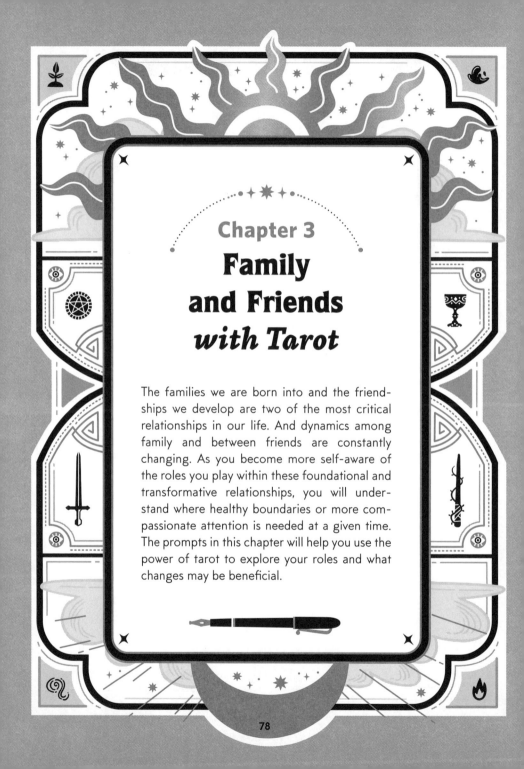

Chapter 3
Family and Friends *with Tarot*

The families we are born into and the friendships we develop are two of the most critical relationships in our life. And dynamics among family and between friends are constantly changing. As you become more self-aware of the roles you play within these foundational and transformative relationships, you will understand where healthy boundaries or more compassionate attention is needed at a given time. The prompts in this chapter will help you use the power of tarot to explore your roles and what changes may be beneficial.

JOURNAL PROMPT

I honor my past in bringing me to my present.

Everyone plays a role in their family unit. Some of those roles are constructive and evolve over time. Other times, a person can be kept static and confined to roles they played as children. Get insight from the keywords of the tarot card you choose to answer this question: How can you describe the roles you currently play in your own family, as well as the part you play in either maintaining or evolving that image?

DATE .... TIME ....

MY CARD ....

CARD TYPE
○ Major Arcana   ○ Minor Arcana

CARD POSITION
○ Upright   ○ Reversed

What feelings came up when I pulled this card?

....
....

What elements of the card's meaning resonate with me and this prompt?

....
....

Which deck did I use? What artwork spoke to me?

....
....

My prompt response and reflections:

....
....
....
....
....
....

Family, however I choose to define it, is important to me.

Tarot can shed light on hidden family dynamics. When you think of the word "family," what do you love and value about this word— because of or in spite of your experiences with family? Use the artwork or keywords of the tarot card you draw for insight and/ or advice into your thoughts and feelings about this word.

DATE .... TIME ....

MY CARD ....

CARD TYPE | CARD POSITION
○ Major Arcana   ○ Minor Arcana | ○ Upright   ○ Reversed

What feelings came up when I pulled this card?

....
....

What elements of the card's meaning resonate with me and this prompt?

....
....

Which deck did I use? What artwork spoke to me?

....
....

My prompt response and reflections:

....
....
....
....
....
....

✦——— **JOURNAL PROMPT** ———✦

I learn from my past relationships with family.

Family dynamics can often present challenges for you to live through
and learn from. What is the most challenging aspect of your family
relationships? Pull a card to understand how you can release this difficulty.

DATE .... TIME ....

MY CARD ....

CARD TYPE
O Major Arcana   O Minor Arcana

CARD POSITION
O Upright   O Reversed

What feelings came up when I pulled this card?

....

....

What elements of the card's meaning resonate with me and this prompt?

....

....

Which deck did I use? What artwork spoke to me?

....

....

My prompt response and reflections:

....

....

....

....

....

....

....

....

JOURNAL PROMPT

My perspective as an individual matters, no matter what my role is in a group.

Families are often best understood by those in them. If you had to describe your family to someone you've never met, how would you do so? Use the card you draw to aid in your understanding of your family and inspire your description.

DATE .... TIME ....

MY CARD ....

CARD TYPE
○ Major Arcana   ○ Minor Arcana

CARD POSITION
○ Upright   ○ Reversed

What feelings came up when I pulled this card?

....

....

What elements of the card's meaning resonate with me and this prompt?

....

....

Which deck did I use? What artwork spoke to me?

....

....

My prompt response and reflections:

....

....

....

....

....

....

....

JOURNAL PROMPT

I honor my roots.

Traditions are a key component of how families relate to one other. Draw a tarot card and meditate on the artwork or the card's keywords to help describe a family tradition that holds a lot of meaning for you, and to better understand what underlying feeling is informing this tradition for you.

DATE .... TIME ....

MY CARD ....

CARD TYPE
○ Major Arcana   ○ Minor Arcana

CARD POSITION
○ Upright   ○ Reversed

What feelings came up when I pulled this card?

....

....

What elements of the card's meaning resonate with me and this prompt?

....

....

Which deck did I use? What artwork spoke to me?

....

....

My prompt response and reflections:

....

....

....

....

....

....

JOURNAL PROMPT

I value my autonomy.

Consider the power of saying no to what you do not want to do. If you are prioritizing other people's needs over your own, whether it's family duties or friendship obligations, use the card you draw to understand where this internalized response comes from within you.

DATE ....   TIME ....

MY CARD ....

CARD TYPE   CARD POSITION
○ Major Arcana   ○ Minor Arcana   ○ Upright   ○ Reversed

What feelings came up when I pulled this card?

....

....

What elements of the card's meaning resonate with me and this prompt?

....

....

Which deck did I use? What artwork spoke to me?

....

....

My prompt response and reflections:

....

....

....

....

....

....

JOURNAL PROMPT

No matter what family I was born into, I can create my own.

Think about what the "perfect" family means to you. Create your own definition, without self-editing or judgment. Using the tarot card you draw, from the artwork or symbolism to the numerology, imagine what having a perfect family would look and feel like to you.

DATE .... TIME ....

MY CARD ....

CARD TYPE
○ Major Arcana   ○ Minor Arcana

CARD POSITION
○ Upright   ○ Reversed

What feelings came up when I pulled this card?

....

....

What elements of the card's meaning resonate with me and this prompt?

....

....

Which deck did I use? What artwork spoke to me?

....

....

My prompt response and reflections:

....

....

....

....

....

....

....

✦ JOURNAL PROMPT ✦

I am aligned and in tune with the truth.

Most families have secrets only known among their members. Carrying the weight of that secret can feel like a burden. Think about a time when you kept a secret—your own or for someone close to you. How did that experience impact you? Was it positive or negative? Draw a tarot card and consider all attributes of that card as you journal about your experience.

DATE .... TIME ....

MY CARD ....

CARD TYPE
○ Major Arcana   ○ Minor Arcana

CARD POSITION
○ Upright   ○ Reversed

What feelings came up when I pulled this card?

....

....

What elements of the card's meaning resonate with me and this prompt?

....

....

Which deck did I use? What artwork spoke to me?

....

....

My prompt response and reflections:

....

....

....

....

....

....

....

+ ——————— **JOURNAL PROMPT** ——————— +

I have compassion for myself because sometimes my friends or family have not been there for me.

Support is an important resource for people to draw from in times of crisis, distress, or confusion. Think of a time when you felt that support was not available or provided by the people you trusted. What did you need to hear at the time? Draw a card guide as the healing message you need to move on from this and journal about the message you receive.

DATE .... TIME ....

MY CARD ....

CARD TYPE
○ Major Arcana   ○ Minor Arcana

CARD POSITION
○ Upright   ○ Reversed

What feelings came up when I pulled this card?

....

....

What elements of the card's meaning resonate with me and this prompt?

....

....

Which deck did I use? What artwork spoke to me?

....

....

My prompt response and reflections:

....

....

....

....

....

....

JOURNAL PROMPT

My friendships uplift and inspire me.

Use the themes, symbolism, keywords, and/or artwork of the card you draw to help you describe what being "a good friend" means to you and all the ways your friendships inspire you.

DATE .... TIME ....

MY CARD ....

CARD TYPE   CARD POSITION
O Major Arcana   O Minor Arcana | O Upright   O Reversed

What feelings came up when I pulled this card?

....
....

What elements of the card's meaning resonate with me and this prompt?

....
....

Which deck did I use? What artwork spoke to me?

....
....

My prompt response and reflections:

....
....
....
....
....
....
....
....
....

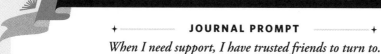
JOURNAL PROMPT

When I need support, I have trusted friends to turn to.

When you think of wise counsel, you can begin to think of your seventy-eight tarot cards as those close friends and confidantes. Like friends, these guides can be there for you and support you even if actual friends and family can't be there. Tell the cards about a secret or a pressing issue. What advice does the card you draw give you about this secret or situation?

DATE .... TIME ....

MY CARD ....

CARD TYPE
O Major Arcana   O Minor Arcana

CARD POSITION
O Upright   O Reversed

What feelings came up when I pulled this card?

....

....

What elements of the card's meaning resonate with me and this prompt?

....

....

Which deck did I use? What artwork spoke to me?

....

....

My prompt response and reflections:

....

....

....

....

....

....

....

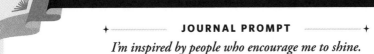
+———— **JOURNAL PROMPT** ————+

I'm inspired by people who encourage me to shine.

Think of a person you feel most at home with or are most yourself with. How do they inspire you to be your best? Who can you be when you don't have to worry that they won't love or accept you? Reflect, then draw a tarot card to answer this question: How does this person see you and what do you represent to them?

DATE .... TIME ....

MY CARD ....

CARD TYPE
○ Major Arcana   ○ Minor Arcana

CARD POSITION
○ Upright   ○ Reversed

What feelings came up when I pulled this card?

....
....

What elements of the card's meaning resonate with me and this prompt?

....
....

Which deck did I use? What artwork spoke to me?

....
....

My prompt response and reflections:

....
....
....
....
....
....
....

JOURNAL PROMPT

I choose my friends for their positive qualities.

Think of your best friend(s). What do you love most about them? Draw a card and use the positive keywords associated with that card to understand what you value most in friendships. Is it trust? Is it fun? Is it celebration?

DATE .... TIME ....

MY CARD ....

CARD TYPE
○ Major Arcana ○ Minor Arcana

CARD POSITION
○ Upright ○ Reversed

What feelings came up when I pulled this card?

....

....

What elements of the card's meaning resonate with me and this prompt?

....

....

Which deck did I use? What artwork spoke to me?

....

....

My prompt response and reflections:

....

....

....

....

....

....

....

+ ——————— **JOURNAL PROMPT** ——————— +

I show up for my friends wholeheartedly, no matter what.

When can being a friend become difficult? What blocks you in those moments? Draw a tarot card to understand another path available to you so you can show up and be supportive when someone needs you to be there for them.

DATE .... TIME ....

MY CARD ....

CARD TYPE   CARD POSITION
O Major Arcana O Minor Arcana | O Upright O Reversed

What feelings came up when I pulled this card?

....

....

What elements of the card's meaning resonate with me and this prompt?

....

....

Which deck did I use? What artwork spoke to me?

....

....

My prompt response and reflections:

....

....

....

....

....

....

JOURNAL PROMPT

I honor my friendships even as they evolve.

Maintaining friendships takes work—just as much as romantic relationships do. As friendships change, you might have to put in even more work. Based on the card you draw, what is something you can do in the next month to invest more time, energy, or effort to show your friends how important they are to you?

DATE .... TIME ....

MY CARD ....

CARD TYPE
O Major Arcana   O Minor Arcana

CARD POSITION
O Upright   O Reversed

What feelings came up when I pulled this card?

....

....

What elements of the card's meaning resonate with me and this prompt?

....

....

Which deck did I use? What artwork spoke to me?

....

....

My prompt response and reflections:

....

....

....

....

....

....

....

+ ──────── **JOURNAL PROMPT** ──────── +

I value the time, energy, and effort I spend with my
friends and that they give back to me.

Between work, school, family obligations, romantic partners, and daily
chores, friendships can fall off your priority list. If you can't give literal
time, what is something you *can* give to let someone know you're
thinking of them? Use the card drawn as guidance in your answer.

DATE .... TIME ....

MY CARD ....

CARD TYPE   CARD POSITION
○ Major Arcana   ○ Minor Arcana   ○ Upright   ○ Reversed

What feelings came up when I pulled this card?

....
....

What elements of the card's meaning resonate with me and this prompt?

....
....

Which deck did I use? What artwork spoke to me?

....
....

My prompt response and reflections:

....
....
....
....
....
....

+ ──────── **JOURNAL PROMPT** ──────── +

As I grow, I understand that my needs for companionship change.

Making friends as you get older can present different challenges from when you were younger. Reflecting on the card you draw, what is something you can do right now to welcome new friends or groups into your circle?

DATE .... TIME ....

MY CARD ....

CARD TYPE
○ Major Arcana   ○ Minor Arcana

CARD POSITION
○ Upright   ○ Reversed

What feelings came up when I pulled this card?

....
....

What elements of the card's meaning resonate with me and this prompt?

....
....

Which deck did I use? What artwork spoke to me?

....
....

My prompt response and reflections:

....
....
....
....
....
....
....

+ ——————— **JOURNAL PROMPT** ——————— +

I welcome opportunities for fun.

Picture the card you draw as a friend you are going to spend the day with. What fun activities are you two doing together? What are you talking about? Wearing? Feeling?

DATE .... TIME ....

MY CARD ....

CARD TYPE ....

○ Major Arcana ○ Minor Arcana

CARD POSITION

○ Upright ○ Reversed

What feelings came up when I pulled this card?

....

....

What elements of the card's meaning resonate with me and this prompt?

....

....

Which deck did I use? What artwork spoke to me?

....

....

My prompt response and reflections:

....

....

....

....

....

....

....

Some of my most cherished memories are moments spent with friends.

Think of a person you miss. Reminisce about some of your favorite memories with this person. According to your chosen card, is there a certain friendship you should spend more time nurturing?

DATE .... TIME ....

MY CARD ....

CARD TYPE   CARD POSITION
O Major Arcana   O Minor Arcana   O Upright   O Reversed

What feelings came up when I pulled this card?

....

....

What elements of the card's meaning resonate with me and this prompt?

....

....

Which deck did I use? What artwork spoke to me?

....

....

My prompt response and reflections:

....

....

....

....

....

....

....

....

JOURNAL PROMPT

I am empowered to reclaim my story.

There are memories that linger. Write a letter to a person whose actions or words hurt you. Use the compassionate wisdom of the tarot card you draw to inform your message to this person— or to yourself as you reflect on how you were hurt.

DATE .... TIME ....

MY CARD ....

CARD TYPE
○ Major Arcana   ○ Minor Arcana

CARD POSITION
○ Upright   ○ Reversed

What feelings came up when I pulled this card?

....
....

What elements of the card's meaning resonate with me and this prompt?

....
....

Which deck did I use? What artwork spoke to me?

....
....

My prompt response and reflections:

....
....
....
....
....
....
....

JOURNAL PROMPT

I want my friendships to be loving and kind.

Even with the best of intentions, there can be misunderstandings between friends—and those can spiral into full-blown arguments. Think of a recent argument you had with someone you care about. If you could do it over again, what would you say differently? What energy can you tap in to, according to the tarot card you draw, to understand how you could handle an argument with a loved one more constructively next time?

DATE .... TIME ....

MY CARD ....

CARD TYPE
O Major Arcana   O Minor Arcana

CARD POSITION
O Upright   O Reversed

What feelings came up when I pulled this card?

....
....

What elements of the card's meaning resonate with me and this prompt?

....
....

Which deck did I use? What artwork spoke to me?

....
....

My prompt response and reflections:

....
....
....
....
....
....

+ ——————— **JOURNAL PROMPT** ——————— +

I make every interaction I have with my loved ones more meaningful.

What would you like your children, the children in your life, or your future children to say about you? Use the tarot to guide your response, using the keywords of that card to uncover something you can further cultivate or release for healing.

DATE .... TIME ....

MY CARD ....

CARD TYPE | CARD POSITION
O Major Arcana   O Minor Arcana | O Upright   O Reversed

What feelings came up when I pulled this card?

....

....

What elements of the card's meaning resonate with me and this prompt?

....

....

Which deck did I use? What artwork spoke to me?

....

....

My prompt response and reflections:

....

....

....

....

....

....

JOURNAL PROMPT

I release relationships that do not align with my present self.

People change—and so do your relationships with them. As you think about a family relationship or friendship that changed or ended in an upsetting way, draw a card to gain more insight into that relationship—and whether it supports your highest good, greater purpose, and personal values.

DATE .... TIME ....

MY CARD ....

CARD TYPE

○ Major Arcana   ○ Minor Arcana

CARD POSITION

○ Upright   ○ Reversed

What feelings came up when I pulled this card?

....

....

What elements of the card's meaning resonate with me and this prompt?

....

....

Which deck did I use? What artwork spoke to me?

....

....

My prompt response and reflections:

....

....

....

....

....

....

....

JOURNAL PROMPT

I cultivate intimacy among my family and friends.

What is one thing you wish you could tell your family or friends, soul to soul? Draw a card to help you find the words you can't say out loud. Journal about how this exercise can help you better communicate your needs—even if you never show them this page—in your next interaction with them.

DATE .... TIME ....

MY CARD ....

CARD TYPE
○ Major Arcana ○ Minor Arcana

CARD POSITION
○ Upright ○ Reversed

What feelings came up when I pulled this card?

....
....

What elements of the card's meaning resonate with me and this prompt?

....
....

Which deck did I use? What artwork spoke to me?

....
....

My prompt response and reflections:

....
....
....
....
....
....

JOURNAL PROMPT

I value my relationships while still honoring everyone's boundaries.

Even the most well-intentioned family and friends can show disregard for your requests. What advice does the card you draw offer about safeguarding your well-being with family or friends who have loose boundaries or who violate your privacy or sense of autonomy?

DATE .... TIME ....

MY CARD ....

CARD TYPE
○ Major Arcana ○ Minor Arcana

CARD POSITION
○ Upright ○ Reversed

What feelings came up when I pulled this card?

....

....

What elements of the card's meaning resonate with me and this prompt?

....

....

Which deck did I use? What artwork spoke to me?

....

....

My prompt response and reflections:

....

....

....

....

....

....

....

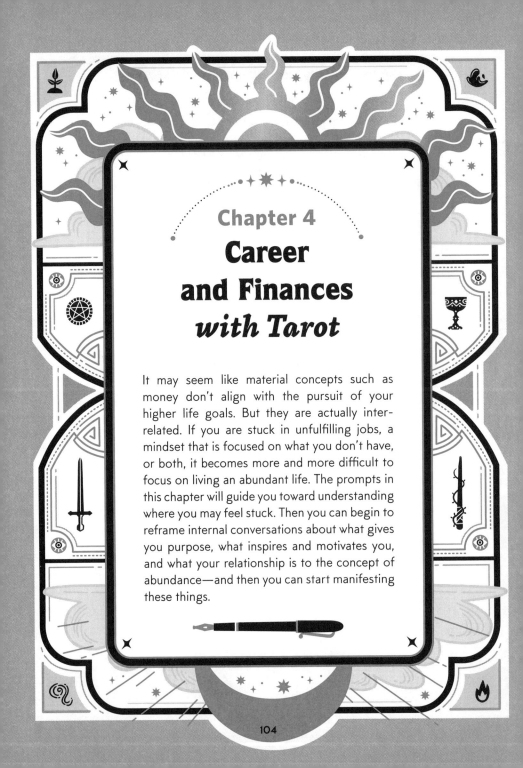

Chapter 4
Career
and Finances
with Tarot

It may seem like material concepts such as money don't align with the pursuit of your higher life goals. But they are actually inter-related. If you are stuck in unfulfilling jobs, a mindset that is focused on what you don't have, or both, it becomes more and more difficult to focus on living an abundant life. The prompts in this chapter will guide you toward understanding where you may feel stuck. Then you can begin to reframe internal conversations about what gives you purpose, what inspires and motivates you, and what your relationship is to the concept of abundance—and then you can start manifesting these things.

JOURNAL PROMPT

I am empowered to live my dreams.

What is your dream job—your true calling? Do you already know?
If so, what can the card you draw show you about that job that you
haven't considered? If you don't know, reflect on what the card
you draw has to say about what your dream job could be.

DATE .... TIME ....

MY CARD ....

CARD TYPE
O Major Arcana   O Minor Arcana

CARD POSITION
O Upright   O Reversed

What feelings came up when I pulled this card?

....
....

What elements of the card's meaning resonate with me and this prompt?

....
....

Which deck did I use? What artwork spoke to me?

....
....

My prompt response and reflections:

....
....
....
....
....
....
....

JOURNAL PROMPT

I take steps to work toward my goals.

Based on the card you draw, what action-oriented step
can you take right now to progress in your career?

DATE .... TIME ....

MY CARD ....

CARD TYPE | CARD POSITION
○ Major Arcana ○ Minor Arcana | ○ Upright ○ Reversed

What feelings came up when I pulled this card?

....

....

What elements of the card's meaning resonate with me and this prompt?

....

....

Which deck did I use? What artwork spoke to me?

....

....

My prompt response and reflections:

....

....

....

....

....

....

....

....

JOURNAL PROMPT

My passions are important to me.

What is your favorite hobby? Draw a card to reveal the link between this hobby and what you do for a living. Are they connected? Would you like them to be? Why or why not?

DATE .... TIME ....

MY CARD ....

CARD TYPE
○ Major Arcana   ○ Minor Arcana

CARD POSITION
○ Upright   ○ Reversed

What feelings came up when I pulled this card?

....

....

What elements of the card's meaning resonate with me and this prompt?

....

....

Which deck did I use? What artwork spoke to me?

....

....

My prompt response and reflections:

....

....

....

....

....

....

....

....

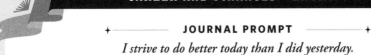
+ ———— **JOURNAL PROMPT** ———— +

I strive to do better today than I did yesterday.

The workplace can bring out innate competitive streaks—within ourselves or within others. What is your relationship to competition? Do you seek it out or avoid it completely? Based on the card you draw, what can you do to improve your relationship to this word—a feeling you can lean into to assert yourself or is there something to release surrounding it?

DATE .... TIME ....

MY CARD ....

CARD TYPE
○ Major Arcana   ○ Minor Arcana

CARD POSITION
○ Upright   ○ Reversed

What feelings came up when I pulled this card?

....
....

What elements of the card's meaning resonate with me and this prompt?

....
....

Which deck did I use? What artwork spoke to me?

....
....

My prompt response and reflections:

....
....
....
....
....
....

✦──────── **JOURNAL PROMPT** ────────✦

I aim to have a job that reflects my greatest desires.

We've all been inspired by someone professionally—a former or current boss, a celebrity or athlete, or someone we follow on social media. Use the tarot card you draw to get insider insight into their work ethic: What is coming through for you? What element is coming up: Swords, for someone who uses their intellect? Wands for creativity?

DATE .... TIME ....

MY CARD ....

CARD TYPE
○ Major Arcana ○ Minor Arcana

CARD POSITION
○ Upright ○ Reversed

What feelings came up when I pulled this card?

....

....

What elements of the card's meaning resonate with me and this prompt?

....

....

Which deck did I use? What artwork spoke to me?

....

....

My prompt response and reflections:

....

....

....

....

....

....

....

✦ ———— **JOURNAL PROMPT** ———— ✦

I acknowledge my mistakes and aim to do better next time.

Everyone has times when they don't give something their all—and know they could've. If you ended the workweek feeling uninspired or like you let a boss or coworker down, draw a card to contextualize the situation. Use the advice of this card to find something constructive that you can do next week to avoid feeling this way again.

DATE .... TIME ....

MY CARD ....

CARD TYPE | CARD POSITION
○ Major Arcana ○ Minor Arcana | ○ Upright ○ Reversed

What feelings came up when I pulled this card?

....

....

What elements of the card's meaning resonate with me and this prompt?

....

....

Which deck did I use? What artwork spoke to me?

....

....

My prompt response and reflections:

....

....

....

....

....

....

....

+ ——————— **JOURNAL PROMPT** ——————— +

I pursue my work with a full heart.

What about your job do you love the most? That you know you're great at? Use the card you draw to reflect on your strengths.

DATE .... TIME ....

MY CARD ....

CARD TYPE
○ Major Arcana   ○ Minor Arcana

CARD POSITION
○ Upright   ○ Reversed

What feelings came up when I pulled this card?

....
....

What elements of the card's meaning resonate with me and this prompt?

....
....

Which deck did I use? What artwork spoke to me?

....
....

My prompt response and reflections:

....
....
....
....
....
....
....
....
....

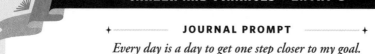

Every day is a day to get one step closer to my goal.

To manifest your dreams, you have to meet the Universe halfway. Meaning, you must take action on your dreams too. What is one thing you can do today to show the Universe you are participating in your dream job manifestation? Use the tarot card you draw to get inspired on what message the Universe is offering on how to meet them in the middle: Is it a mindset shift? Is it a specific action?

DATE .... TIME ....

MY CARD ....

CARD TYPE   CARD POSITION
○ Major Arcana   ○ Minor Arcana | ○ Upright   ○ Reversed

What feelings came up when I pulled this card?

....

....

What elements of the card's meaning resonate with me and this prompt?

....

....

Which deck did I use? What artwork spoke to me?

....

....

My prompt response and reflections:

....

....

....

....

....

....

✦————— **JOURNAL PROMPT** —————✦

I am open to changes that serve my highest good.

Changes in careers can happen—sometimes intentionally, sometimes unexpectedly. What does the card you pull say about the next phase of your career? What does it look and feel like? Is it showing that there is something you can do right now to prepare for the change?

DATE .... TIME ....

MY CARD ....

CARD TYPE
O Major Arcana   O Minor Arcana

CARD POSITION
O Upright   O Reversed

What feelings came up when I pulled this card?

....
....

What elements of the card's meaning resonate with me and this prompt?

....
....

Which deck did I use? What artwork spoke to me?

....
....

My prompt response and reflections:

....
....
....
....
....
....
....

✦ ——————— **JOURNAL PROMPT** ——————— ✦

I am proud of my accomplishments.

What do you consider to be your greatest career achievement? What insight can the card you draw show you about this moment?

DATE .... TIME ....

MY CARD ....

CARD TYPE
○ Major Arcana ○ Minor Arcana

CARD POSITION
○ Upright ○ Reversed

What feelings came up when I pulled this card?

....

....

What elements of the card's meaning resonate with me and this prompt?

....

....

Which deck did I use? What artwork spoke to me?

....

....

My prompt response and reflections:

....

....

....

....

....

....

....

....

My professional relationships are important to me.

Depending on the type of career or job you are in, you can end up spending a lot of time with your colleagues. And while you can't control other people's behavior, you are always in charge of your own. Based on the card you draw, what do you think your coworkers would say is the best part of working with you?

DATE .... TIME ....

MY CARD ....

CARD TYPE
O Major Arcana   O Minor Arcana

CARD POSITION
O Upright   O Reversed

What feelings came up when I pulled this card?

....

....

What elements of the card's meaning resonate with me and this prompt?

....

....

Which deck did I use? What artwork spoke to me?

....

....

My prompt response and reflections:

....

....

....

....

....

....

JOURNAL PROMPT

I value my free time as much as my work time.

Picture never having to work another day in your life. What kind of feelings does that bring up for you? Use keywords and/or symbols from the card you draw to guide your reflection on whether you view this positively or find the idea uncomfortable. Explore why.

DATE .... TIME ....

MY CARD ....

CARD TYPE   CARD POSITION
○ Major Arcana ○ Minor Arcana   ○ Upright ○ Reversed

What feelings came up when I pulled this card?

....

....

What elements of the card's meaning resonate with me and this prompt?

....

....

Which deck did I use? What artwork spoke to me?

....

....

My prompt response and reflections:

....

....

....

....

....

....

JOURNAL PROMPT

I accept constructive feedback with grace.

Write a career performance review of yourself from the perspective of the card you draw. What would that card say to you if they were sitting across from you? Would they emphasize your strengths or areas for improvement? Think about what our inner voice projects outward as you do this. This card can help you unpack what kind of self-talk, positive or negative, is influencing you on a subconscious level.

DATE .... TIME ....

MY CARD ....

CARD TYPE
O Major Arcana O Minor Arcana

CARD POSITION
O Upright O Reversed

What feelings came up when I pulled this card?

....
....

What elements of the card's meaning resonate with me and this prompt?

....
....

Which deck did I use? What artwork spoke to me?

....
....

My prompt response and reflections:

....
....
....
....
....
....

JOURNAL PROMPT
My life is abundant.

What does the concept of abundance mean to you? How might the card you draw show new ways to welcome more financial abundance into your life?

DATE .... TIME ....

MY CARD ....

CARD TYPE
O Major Arcana   O Minor Arcana

CARD POSITION
O Upright   O Reversed

What feelings came up when I pulled this card?

....

....

What elements of the card's meaning resonate with me and this prompt?

....

....

Which deck did I use? What artwork spoke to me?

....

....

My prompt response and reflections:

....

....

....

....

....

....

....

....

....

+ ———— **JOURNAL PROMPT** ———— +

I am improving my relationship to money.

Fill in the blank: "When I look at my bank account, I feel
_____." Use the card you draw to guide you as you
answer this and explore the reasoning behind your feelings.

DATE .... TIME ....

MY CARD ....

CARD TYPE
O Major Arcana   O Minor Arcana

CARD POSITION
O Upright   O Reversed

What feelings came up when I pulled this card?

....

....

What elements of the card's meaning resonate with me and this prompt?

....

....

Which deck did I use? What artwork spoke to me?

....

....

My prompt response and reflections:

....

....

....

....

....

....

....

....

JOURNAL PROMPT

Security and stability are important to me.

When you feel a lack of financial security, what is your reaction? Describe the feeling. Then use the card you draw to help you release these feelings, using its message to you as a way to gain insight on how to feel more empowered.

DATE .... TIME ....

MY CARD ....

CARD TYPE
○ Major Arcana   ○ Minor Arcana

CARD POSITION
○ Upright   ○ Reversed

What feelings came up when I pulled this card?

....
....

What elements of the card's meaning resonate with me and this prompt?

....
....

Which deck did I use? What artwork spoke to me?

....
....

My prompt response and reflections:

....
....
....
....
....
....
....
....

JOURNAL PROMPT

I take control of my future.

What is one thing that the card you draw can show you about how to improve your relationship with the concept of wealth (that is not just about finances)? How can this help you to feel more in control of your future?

DATE .... TIME ....

MY CARD ....

CARD TYPE
○ Major Arcana   ○ Minor Arcana

CARD POSITION
○ Upright   ○ Reversed

What feelings came up when I pulled this card?

What elements of the card's meaning resonate with me and this prompt?

Which deck did I use? What artwork spoke to me?

My prompt response and reflections:

JOURNAL PROMPT
Treating myself is important.

Think about the most expensive thing you've ever purchased for yourself. What feeling comes up when you think about it? What can the card you draw show you about that experience?

DATE .... TIME ....

MY CARD ....

CARD TYPE
○ Major Arcana   ○ Minor Arcana

CARD POSITION
○ Upright   ○ Reversed

What feelings came up when I pulled this card?

....

....

What elements of the card's meaning resonate with me and this prompt?

....

....

Which deck did I use? What artwork spoke to me?

....

....

My prompt response and reflections:

....

....

....

....

....

....

....

JOURNAL PROMPT

The best experiences in life are free.

According to the card you draw, what is one thing you can do today that will not cost any money but will bring a lot of joy?

DATE .... TIME ....

MY CARD ....

CARD TYPE
○ Major Arcana   ○ Minor Arcana

CARD POSITION
○ Upright   ○ Reversed

What feelings came up when I pulled this card?

....

....

What elements of the card's meaning resonate with me and this prompt?

....

....

Which deck did I use? What artwork spoke to me?

....

....

My prompt response and reflections:

....

....

....

....

....

....

....

....

I admire people who go after their dreams.

Fill in the blank: "When I think of a successful person, what I admire most is _____." Use the card you draw to explore similarities between you and this person that you can tap in to right now.

DATE .... TIME ....

MY CARD ....

CARD TYPE
○ Major Arcana   ○ Minor Arcana

CARD POSITION
○ Upright   ○ Reversed

What feelings came up when I pulled this card?

....
....

What elements of the card's meaning resonate with me and this prompt?

....
....

Which deck did I use? What artwork spoke to me?

....
....

My prompt response and reflections:

....
....
....
....
....
....
....

JOURNAL PROMPT

I want to work to live, not live to work.

Consider your current work-life balance. Where on the spectrum do you fall? Do you want to attain more balance? What can the card you draw tell you about what a healthy balance would look like?

DATE .... TIME ....

MY CARD ....

CARD TYPE
○ Major Arcana   ○ Minor Arcana

CARD POSITION
○ Upright   ○ Reversed

What feelings came up when I pulled this card?

....

....

What elements of the card's meaning resonate with me and this prompt?

....

....

Which deck did I use? What artwork spoke to me?

....

....

My prompt response and reflections:

....

....

....

....

....

....

....

....

JOURNAL PROMPT

I can have the career I've always imagined.

Using the themes, keywords, and symbolism of the card you draw, imagine an alternate-universe version of yourself. What is this person doing right now? Where do they work? Based on this image, what is your subconscious trying to tell you about your own career desires in your present day?

DATE .... TIME ....

MY CARD ....

CARD TYPE
○ Major Arcana ○ Minor Arcana

CARD POSITION
○ Upright ○ Reversed

What feelings came up when I pulled this card?

....
....

What elements of the card's meaning resonate with me and this prompt?

....
....

Which deck did I use? What artwork spoke to me?

....
....

My prompt response and reflections:

....
....
....
....
....
....

── ✦ ── **JOURNAL PROMPT** ── ✦ ──

I am the master of my own destiny.

When you think about starting your own business or working for yourself, what feeling does that create? Excitement or anxiety? A combination of both? Draw a card to see what advice the tarot offers about starting your own business and whether you're emotionally and financially ready for this life change.

DATE .... TIME ....

MY CARD ....

CARD TYPE
○ Major Arcana ○ Minor Arcana

CARD POSITION
○ Upright ○ Reversed

What feelings came up when I pulled this card?

....
....

What elements of the card's meaning resonate with me and this prompt?

....
....

Which deck did I use? What artwork spoke to me?

....
....

My prompt response and reflections:

....
....
....
....
....
....
....

JOURNAL PROMPT

I am confident about my choices.

Think about the following scenario: You have two equally viable career paths in front of you. You are not sure which one to choose. Draw a card to help you determine which choice is more in alignment with your current goals.

DATE .... TIME ....

MY CARD ....

CARD TYPE
○ Major Arcana   ○ Minor Arcana

CARD POSITION
○ Upright   ○ Reversed

What feelings came up when I pulled this card?

....

....

What elements of the card's meaning resonate with me and this prompt?

....

....

Which deck did I use? What artwork spoke to me?

....

....

My prompt response and reflections:

....

....

....

....

....

....

....

✦————— **JOURNAL PROMPT** —————✦

I make the best choices I can, given the information
I have available to me at the time.

Use the card you draw to reflect on the following scenario: You have
two viable options in front of you for investing in your financial future.
You chose one, as represented by the card you draw. Are you happy
about it? Conflicted? Filled with longing for the other option?

DATE .... TIME ....

MY CARD ....

CARD TYPE | CARD POSITION
○ Major Arcana   ○ Minor Arcana | ○ Upright   ○ Reversed

What feelings came up when I pulled this card?

....

....

What elements of the card's meaning resonate with me and this prompt?

....

....

Which deck did I use? What artwork spoke to me?

....

....

My prompt response and reflections:

....

....

....

....

....

....

....

Chapter 5
Health and Body *with Tarot*

Your body is a crucial part of manifesting purpose and growth. The choice to live in your body, navigate its changes over time, and address its challenges or strengths is connected to your growth and development as a person. Equally important is nurturing your mental well-being, as a vital part of your health (however intangible it may be). The prompts in this chapter are designed to help you gain a greater understanding and appreciation for the amazing body that carries you—physically and mentally—through life.

◆──────── **JOURNAL PROMPT** ────────◆

I value my physical form, even what I perceive as its flaws.

Use the card you draw to guide you as you write a gratitude letter to your body. Work keywords attached to this card into your letter.

DATE .... TIME ....

MY CARD ....

CARD TYPE
○ Major Arcana   ○ Minor Arcana

CARD POSITION
○ Upright   ○ Reversed

What feelings came up when I pulled this card?

....

....

What elements of the card's meaning resonate with me and this prompt?

....

....

Which deck did I use? What artwork spoke to me?

....

....

My prompt response and reflections:

....

....

....

....

....

....

....

....

....

JOURNAL PROMPT

I honor my mental well-being.

Under times of stress, we all have certain coping mechanisms. Can you identify what yours are? What can the tarot show you about how helpful those strategies may or may not be to your mental health?

DATE .... TIME ....

MY CARD ....

CARD TYPE
○ Major Arcana ○ Minor Arcana

CARD POSITION
○ Upright ○ Reversed

What feelings came up when I pulled this card?

....
....

What elements of the card's meaning resonate with me and this prompt?

....
....

Which deck did I use? What artwork spoke to me?

....
....

My prompt response and reflections:

....
....
....
....
....
....
....
....

+ ──────── **JOURNAL PROMPT** ──────── +

I am in tune with my body and its changes.

Like the signs and symbols all around you, your body is always sending you messages. Draw a tarot card to receive a message about something your body needs from you right now. This could be emotional, mental, or physical sustenance.

DATE .... TIME ....

MY CARD ....

CARD TYPE
○ Major Arcana   ○ Minor Arcana

CARD POSITION
○ Upright   ○ Reversed

What feelings came up when I pulled this card?

....

....

What elements of the card's meaning resonate with me and this prompt?

....

....

Which deck did I use? What artwork spoke to me?

....

....

My prompt response and reflections:

....

....

....

....

....

....

....

JOURNAL PROMPT

I love my body.

Think about a perceived flaw or physical insecurity you have.
Instead of wishing to change it, what if you were forced to think
the opposite about it—at least for the length of this prompt.
How can the insight and keywords of the card you draw help
you reframe what you say to yourself about your body?

DATE ....   TIME ....

MY CARD ....

CARD TYPE | CARD POSITION
○ Major Arcana   ○ Minor Arcana | ○ Upright   ○ Reversed

What feelings came up when I pulled this card?

....
....

What elements of the card's meaning resonate with me and this prompt?

....
....

Which deck did I use? What artwork spoke to me?

....
....

My prompt response and reflections:

....
....
....
....
....
....
....

JOURNAL PROMPT

I love myself, especially during difficult days.

Everyone has bad or "blah" days. Write a love letter to yourself from the perspective of the card you draw. What can this card see about you that you don't? Is there a person depicted on this card? Is there a symbol? What about the card's keyword? Meditate on the positive attributes of this card's symbolism or artwork. Include something positive about this day.

DATE .... TIME ....

MY CARD ....

CARD TYPE
○ Major Arcana   ○ Minor Arcana

CARD POSITION
○ Upright   ○ Reversed

What feelings came up when I pulled this card?

....

....

What elements of the card's meaning resonate with me and this prompt?

....

....

Which deck did I use? What artwork spoke to me?

....

....

My prompt response and reflections:

....

....

....

....

....

....

....

JOURNAL PROMPT

I cultivate a healthy curiosity about myself.

What emotion or emotions are you currently experiencing? Is it a comfortable experience or overwhelming? Draw a card and see what comes up for you about the root emotion you are being invited to focus on right now.

DATE .... TIME ....

MY CARD ....

CARD TYPE
○ Major Arcana   ○ Minor Arcana

CARD POSITION
○ Upright   ○ Reversed

What feelings came up when I pulled this card?

....

....

What elements of the card's meaning resonate with me and this prompt?

....

....

Which deck did I use? What artwork spoke to me?

....

....

My prompt response and reflections:

....

....

....

....

....

....

....

JOURNAL PROMPT

My physical body is part of this earth.

Take a walk today or get outside in nature in some other way.
Make a deliberate intention to commune with the physical world.
Before you go, draw a card and see what symbols or keywords
come forward. After getting into nature, reflect on whether you
encountered those symbols or keywords during your experience.

DATE .... TIME ....

MY CARD ....

CARD TYPE
○ Major Arcana   ○ Minor Arcana

CARD POSITION
○ Upright   ○ Reversed

What feelings came up when I pulled this card?

....

....

What elements of the card's meaning resonate with me and this prompt?

....

....

Which deck did I use? What artwork spoke to me?

....

....

My prompt response and reflections:

....

....

....

....

....

....

....

+ ———— **JOURNAL PROMPT** ———— +

I release stressful situations I cannot control.

When you think about what stresses you out mentally or
physically, what energy does the card you draw offer for you
to tap in to when you are starting to feel overwhelmed?

DATE .... TIME ....

MY CARD ....

CARD TYPE

○ Major Arcana ○ Minor Arcana

CARD POSITION

○ Upright ○ Reversed

What feelings came up when I pulled this card?

....

....

What elements of the card's meaning resonate with me and this prompt?

....

....

Which deck did I use? What artwork spoke to me?

....

....

My prompt response and reflections:

....

....

....

....

....

....

....

JOURNAL PROMPT

I am both spirit and body: There is no divide.

In your journey to love your body more, what does the card you draw indicate about what you can actively do to increase your physical engagement with the world around you? Use this card's insight to help increase your awareness of the connection between your body and your spirit.

DATE .... TIME ....

MY CARD ....

CARD TYPE
○ Major Arcana ○ Minor Arcana

CARD POSITION
○ Upright ○ Reversed

What feelings came up when I pulled this card?

....

....

What elements of the card's meaning resonate with me and this prompt?

....

....

Which deck did I use? What artwork spoke to me?

....

....

My prompt response and reflections:

....

....

....

....

....

....

JOURNAL PROMPT

I am an energetic being.

Think about where you expend the most energy: Are you physically on the verge of burnout through overexertion? Staying up too late? Or do you spend a lot of mental energy worrying? Draw a tarot card to understand what energetic realm is currently sapping you of your strength and how you can release it.

DATE .... TIME ....

MY CARD ....

CARD TYPE
○ Major Arcana ○ Minor Arcana

CARD POSITION
○ Upright ○ Reversed

What feelings came up when I pulled this card?

....

....

What elements of the card's meaning resonate with me and this prompt?

....

....

Which deck did I use? What artwork spoke to me?

....

....

My prompt response and reflections:

....

....

....

....

....

....

JOURNAL PROMPT

I face my fears with courage.

Think about something you're afraid of or that creates a sense of trepidation in you. How can the tarot help you face or release this fear in order to maintain a more balanced state of mental well-being?

DATE .... TIME ....

MY CARD ....

CARD TYPE
○ Major Arcana   ○ Minor Arcana

CARD POSITION
○ Upright   ○ Reversed

What feelings came up when I pulled this card?

....

....

What elements of the card's meaning resonate with me and this prompt?

....

....

Which deck did I use? What artwork spoke to me?

....

....

My prompt response and reflections:

....

....

....

....

....

....

....

JOURNAL PROMPT

I release habits that hinder my growth.

Do you currently have any habits that may have been a helpful coping mechanism at one time, but now impact your health negatively? Ask the tarot to help show you what habit is holding you back—and the underlying feeling that may be triggering it.

DATE .... TIME ....

MY CARD ....

CARD TYPE   CARD POSITION
O Major Arcana   O Minor Arcana   O Upright   O Reversed

What feelings came up when I pulled this card?

....

....

What elements of the card's meaning resonate with me and this prompt?

....

....

Which deck did I use? What artwork spoke to me?

....

....

My prompt response and reflections:

....

....

....

....

....

....

JOURNAL PROMPT

I release thought patterns that hold me back.

Do you currently hold any self-limiting beliefs about your body?
Use the themes, keywords, and symbolism of the card you draw
to help shed or reframe any negative self-talk that could be
holding you back from loving and appreciating yourself.

DATE .... TIME ....

MY CARD ....

CARD TYPE   CARD POSITION
○ Major Arcana   ○ Minor Arcana   ○ Upright   ○ Reversed

What feelings came up when I pulled this card?

What elements of the card's meaning resonate with me and this prompt?

Which deck did I use? What artwork spoke to me?

My prompt response and reflections:

JOURNAL PROMPT

I surround myself with positivity.

Think about the last show you watched, song or podcast you listened to, or book you read. Did it leave you feeling happy and inspired or scared and/or pessimistic? Draw a card to better understand how your interactions with these mediums impact your mental health.

DATE .... TIME ....

MY CARD ....

CARD TYPE
○ Major Arcana   ○ Minor Arcana

CARD POSITION
○ Upright   ○ Reversed

What feelings came up when I pulled this card?

....

....

What elements of the card's meaning resonate with me and this prompt?

....

....

Which deck did I use? What artwork spoke to me?

....

....

My prompt response and reflections:

....

....

....

....

....

....

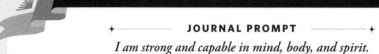
+ ———— **JOURNAL PROMPT** ———— +

I am strong and capable in mind, body, and spirit.

Belief in your own capabilities extends beyond the physical. Your
personal beliefs can shape how you see yourself and the world. What
are you capable of that you don't currently see or fully appreciate
about yourself? Draw a tarot card to discover the answer.

DATE .... TIME ....

MY CARD ....

CARD TYPE
○ Major Arcana   ○ Minor Arcana

CARD POSITION
○ Upright   ○ Reversed

What feelings came up when I pulled this card?

....

....

What elements of the card's meaning resonate with me and this prompt?

....

....

Which deck did I use? What artwork spoke to me?

....

....

My prompt response and reflections:

....

....

....

....

....

....

✦ ──── JOURNAL PROMPT ──── ✦

My imagination is vivid and fun.

If the limits of the human body did not exist, what would you want to be able to do and why? Use the card you draw to open your mind up to imaginative possibilities.

DATE .... TIME ....

MY CARD ....

CARD TYPE
O Major Arcana   O Minor Arcana

CARD POSITION
O Upright   O Reversed

What feelings came up when I pulled this card?

....

....

What elements of the card's meaning resonate with me and this prompt?

....

....

Which deck did I use? What artwork spoke to me?

....

....

My prompt response and reflections:

....

....

....

....

....

....

....

JOURNAL PROMPT

I trust my body.

Think of a time when a thought or movement made you feel strong, powerful, or proud. What further insight about your body can you gather from the card you draw about this memory?

DATE .... TIME ....

MY CARD ....

CARD TYPE
○ Major Arcana   ○ Minor Arcana

CARD POSITION
○ Upright   ○ Reversed

What feelings came up when I pulled this card?

....

....

What elements of the card's meaning resonate with me and this prompt?

....

....

Which deck did I use? What artwork spoke to me?

....

....

My prompt response and reflections:

....

....

....

....

....

....

....

+ ——— **JOURNAL PROMPT** ——— +

I take care of my body from the inside out.

How do you define self-care? How do you practice it? Use the card you draw to determine your next self-care activity so you can better align to a balanced mind-body-spirit connection.

DATE .... TIME ....

MY CARD ....

CARD TYPE
○ Major Arcana ○ Minor Arcana

CARD POSITION
○ Upright ○ Reversed

What feelings came up when I pulled this card?

....
....

What elements of the card's meaning resonate with me and this prompt?

....
....

Which deck did I use? What artwork spoke to me?

....
....

My prompt response and reflections:

....
....
....
....
....
....
....
....

JOURNAL PROMPT

Adventure is how I define it.

If you could do anything today, absent of responsibilities or restrictions, what would it be? What does the card you draw show you about this desire, and what makes you feel adventurous?

DATE .... TIME ....

MY CARD ....

CARD TYPE
O Major Arcana   O Minor Arcana

CARD POSITION
O Upright   O Reversed

What feelings came up when I pulled this card?

....

....

What elements of the card's meaning resonate with me and this prompt?

....

....

Which deck did I use? What artwork spoke to me?

....

....

My prompt response and reflections:

....

....

....

....

....

....

....

....

JOURNAL PROMPT
I value rest.

When you think of resting, what runs through your mind? Does it feel relaxing, or does it feel like you're being unproductive or lazy? What can the card you draw show you about how resting your mind and body can actually help you align to your material goals?

DATE ....   TIME ....

MY CARD ....

CARD TYPE
○ Major Arcana   ○ Minor Arcana

CARD POSITION
○ Upright   ○ Reversed

What feelings came up when I pulled this card?

What elements of the card's meaning resonate with me and this prompt?

Which deck did I use? What artwork spoke to me?

My prompt response and reflections:

+ ———— **JOURNAL PROMPT** ———— +

I am aware of the power of the present moment.

You can rush through your days, from one errand to the next. When viewed cumulatively, it can feel like you are rushing through life. Draw a tarot card to ground you in the present moment. Use the card's artwork or symbolism to find something sensorial—taste, smell, sound, sight, touch—that you can experience right now.

DATE .... TIME ....

MY CARD ....

CARD TYPE
○ Major Arcana   ○ Minor Arcana

CARD POSITION
○ Upright   ○ Reversed

What feelings came up when I pulled this card?

....

....

What elements of the card's meaning resonate with me and this prompt?

....

....

Which deck did I use? What artwork spoke to me?

....

....

My prompt response and reflections:

....

....

....

....

....

....

JOURNAL PROMPT

I am unafraid to let others see me.

Think of a moment you felt shy. That experience left you with symptoms that were of a physical, mental, and emotional nature. What can this experience of fear of intimacy or vulnerability with others show you about yourself? Use the insights from the card you draw to help you face a situation that inspires insecurity with more confidence.

DATE .... TIME ....

MY CARD ....

CARD TYPE
○ Major Arcana ○ Minor Arcana

CARD POSITION
○ Upright ○ Reversed

What feelings came up when I pulled this card?

....

....

What elements of the card's meaning resonate with me and this prompt?

....

....

Which deck did I use? What artwork spoke to me?

....

....

My prompt response and reflections:

....

....

....

....

....

....

Physical pleasure is an important soulful experience.

Based on the card you draw, what is something you can indulge in today to increase your awareness of physical joy?

DATE .... TIME ....

MY CARD ....

CARD TYPE
O Major Arcana   O Minor Arcana

CARD POSITION
O Upright   O Reversed

What feelings came up when I pulled this card?

....
....

What elements of the card's meaning resonate with me and this prompt?

....
....

Which deck did I use? What artwork spoke to me?

....
....

My prompt response and reflections:

....
....
....
....
....
....
....
....

JOURNAL PROMPT

I share my love with others.

Love can be a physical act of service. Think of a time when you provided assistance to someone in physical or mental need. Reflect on how that experience felt. Then draw a tarot card to represent the energy you embodied in this scenario. How does the tarot card you chose reflect the role you played in that moment? Does it change your relationship to or perception of this card?

DATE .... TIME ....

MY CARD ....

CARD TYPE
○ Major Arcana   ○ Minor Arcana

CARD POSITION
○ Upright   ○ Reversed

What feelings came up when I pulled this card?

....

....

What elements of the card's meaning resonate with me and this prompt?

....

....

Which deck did I use? What artwork spoke to me?

....

....

My prompt response and reflections:

....

....

....

....

....

....

+ ──────── **JOURNAL PROMPT** ──────── +

I do not judge myself for difficult emotions—and neither does my tarot deck.

Think about an emotion that is considered uncomfortable or something to avoid. Is it sadness, grief, anger, fear, jealousy? Often, you are told these feelings are "bad" or shameful. According to the card you draw, what is a positive way to improve your relationship with difficult emotions to promote better mental well-being?

DATE .... TIME ....

MY CARD ....

CARD TYPE
O Major Arcana O Minor Arcana

CARD POSITION
O Upright O Reversed

What feelings came up when I pulled this card?

....

....

What elements of the card's meaning resonate with me and this prompt?

....

....

Which deck did I use? What artwork spoke to me?

....

....

My prompt response and reflections:

....

....

....

....

....

....

....

Chapter 6
Spiritual Development *with Tarot*

As you develop your relationship with tarot, your mind will open up to all the possibilities of the Universe, as well as to how tarot is making its presence known in your life. You will begin to really understand that signs and synchronicities are not random. They are not just chance. And the more you notice them, the stronger they become. These journal prompts will help you get aligned—body, mind, and soul—with the messages constantly being sent your way.

+ ——————— **JOURNAL PROMPT** ——————— +

My relationship with tarot is strong and supportive.

As you strengthen your relationship with tarot, you can also grow an individual relationship with specific cards. To do so, reflect on the following when you draw a card: "The reason this card makes me feel [insert a feeling here, like anxious, uncomfortable, hopeful, excited, validated, etc.] is because _____." This exercise can be repeated every time you draw a card.

DATE .... TIME ....

MY CARD ....

CARD TYPE
O Major Arcana   O Minor Arcana

CARD POSITION
O Upright   O Reversed

What feelings came up when I pulled this card?

....

....

What elements of the card's meaning resonate with me and this prompt?

....

....

Which deck did I use? What artwork spoke to me?

....

....

My prompt response and reflections:

....

....

....

....

....

....

JOURNAL PROMPT

I trust my intuition.

Reflect with an open mind about how the card you draw will manifest in your day. This prompt is an invitation to be open-minded to symbolism while honing your intuition. Come back to this journal entry at the end of the day and write about what happened and how it did—or did not—fit the card's traditional meaning.

DATE .... TIME ....

MY CARD ....

CARD TYPE
○ Major Arcana   ○ Minor Arcana

CARD POSITION
○ Upright   ○ Reversed

What feelings came up when I pulled this card?

....
....

What elements of the card's meaning resonate with me and this prompt?

....
....

Which deck did I use? What artwork spoke to me?

....
....

My prompt response and reflections:

....
....
....
....
....
....
....

JOURNAL PROMPT

I thank the Universe for guiding me on my spiritual journey.

What message does your inner self have for you? Draw a tarot card to receive specific advice from the Universe about the energy you can best tap in to at this moment in time.

DATE .... TIME ....

MY CARD ....

CARD TYPE
○ Major Arcana ○ Minor Arcana

CARD POSITION
○ Upright ○ Reversed

What feelings came up when I pulled this card?

....
....

What elements of the card's meaning resonate with me and this prompt?

....
....

Which deck did I use? What artwork spoke to me?

....
....

My prompt response and reflections:

....
....
....
....
....
....
....

+ ———— **JOURNAL PROMPT** ———— +

I accomplish my goals easily.

We all want to know that our life has a deeper meaning. Getting confirmation that you are on the right path and fulfilling your purpose is very affirming. Draw a card as a representation of where you are in your spiritual journey. What does the card you draw have to say about what you can do—or release—to advance in this journey?

DATE .... TIME ....

MY CARD ....

CARD TYPE
○ Major Arcana   ○ Minor Arcana

CARD POSITION
○ Upright   ○ Reversed

What feelings came up when I pulled this card?

....

....

What elements of the card's meaning resonate with me and this prompt?

....

....

Which deck did I use? What artwork spoke to me?

....

....

My prompt response and reflections:

....

....

....

....

....

....

....

JOURNAL PROMPT

I strive to be at peace with myself.

According to the card you draw, what energy might be holding you back from achieving peace? Is it coming from an internal or external force? Use the card you draw for insight on a potential blockage and also the remedy available to you.

DATE .... TIME ....

MY CARD ....

CARD TYPE
○ Major Arcana ○ Minor Arcana

CARD POSITION
○ Upright ○ Reversed

What feelings came up when I pulled this card?

....
....

What elements of the card's meaning resonate with me and this prompt?

....
....

Which deck did I use? What artwork spoke to me?

....
....

My prompt response and reflections:

....
....
....
....
....
....
....

JOURNAL PROMPT

I seek joy for my soul, always.

Brainstorm at least three ways the card you draw is
instructing you to pursue more joy in your life.

DATE .... TIME ....

MY CARD ....

CARD TYPE

○ Major Arcana   ○ Minor Arcana

CARD POSITION

○ Upright   ○ Reversed

What feelings came up when I pulled this card?

....
....

What elements of the card's meaning resonate with me and this prompt?

....
....

Which deck did I use? What artwork spoke to me?

....
....

My prompt response and reflections:

....
....
....
....
....
....
....
....

+──── **JOURNAL PROMPT** ────+

I look ahead with true hope.

What is coming up for you in the card you draw that you can look forward
to most? List at least three possible manifestations of this card's divinatory
possibilities. Then come back to this prompt in a designated time frame
and reflect on how your initial reflections relate to what happened.

DATE .... TIME ....

MY CARD ....

CARD TYPE
○ Major Arcana   ○ Minor Arcana

CARD POSITION
○ Upright   ○ Reversed

What feelings came up when I pulled this card?

....
....

What elements of the card's meaning resonate with me and this prompt?

....
....

Which deck did I use? What artwork spoke to me?

....
....

My prompt response and reflections:

....
....
....
....
....
....

+ ———— **JOURNAL PROMPT** ———— +

I am open to what the Divine wants me to release or make room for.

It is important to remember that your spiritual path is not a destination but a lifelong commitment. You are constantly growing. According to the card you draw, what changes or steps can you take right now to continue growing on your spiritual path to fulfill your sense of purpose?

DATE .... TIME ....

MY CARD ....

CARD TYPE
O Major Arcana   O Minor Arcana

CARD POSITION
O Upright   O Reversed

What feelings came up when I pulled this card?

....

....

What elements of the card's meaning resonate with me and this prompt?

....

....

Which deck did I use? What artwork spoke to me?

....

....

My prompt response and reflections:

....

....

....

....

....

....

+ ———— JOURNAL PROMPT ———— +
Self-care is spiritual.

According to the card you draw, what nurturing can you give your soul right now to enhance your relationship with the powers that be?

DATE .... TIME ....

MY CARD ....

CARD TYPE
O Major Arcana   O Minor Arcana

CARD POSITION
O Upright   O Reversed

What feelings came up when I pulled this card?

....
....

What elements of the card's meaning resonate with me and this prompt?

....
....

Which deck did I use? What artwork spoke to me?

....
....

My prompt response and reflections:

....
....
....
....
....
....
....
....
....

+ ———— **JOURNAL PROMPT** ———— +

My dreams are also a way for me to commune with
the Divine and my own subconscious.

Answer this prompt before a nap, mindful meditation, or bedtime:
"As I fall asleep, what symbol(s) from the card I draw might work
its way into my dream realm, either literally or symbolically?"
Journal about your experience once you wake up.

DATE .... TIME ....

MY CARD ....

CARD TYPE | CARD POSITION
○ Major Arcana   ○ Minor Arcana | ○ Upright   ○ Reversed

What feelings came up when I pulled this card?

....

....

What elements of the card's meaning resonate with me and this prompt?

....

....

Which deck did I use? What artwork spoke to me?

....

....

My prompt response and reflections:

....

....

....

....

....

....

JOURNAL PROMPT

My experiences are valuable teachers.

It is said that most advice people give is autobiographical (learned through personal experience). Consider the possible autobiography of the card you draw. Then reflect on what advice this card would give you based on its experiences.

DATE .... TIME ....

MY CARD ....

CARD TYPE
○ Major Arcana   ○ Minor Arcana

CARD POSITION
○ Upright   ○ Reversed

What feelings came up when I pulled this card?

....

....

What elements of the card's meaning resonate with me and this prompt?

....

....

Which deck did I use? What artwork spoke to me?

....

....

My prompt response and reflections:

....

....

....

....

....

....

....

+ —————— **JOURNAL PROMPT** —————— +

I trust my instincts when something doesn't feel true.

Consider the previous exercise again. As you draw a card, think about the worst advice this card could give you. Reflect on why it feels untrue and where you store that feeling in your body. This exercise is a good lesson in trusting your instincts and knowing when something being said to you is not aligned with your inner truth.

DATE .... TIME ....

MY CARD ....

CARD TYPE
○ Major Arcana ○ Minor Arcana

CARD POSITION
○ Upright ○ Reversed

What feelings came up when I pulled this card?

....

....

What elements of the card's meaning resonate with me and this prompt?

....

....

Which deck did I use? What artwork spoke to me?

....

....

My prompt response and reflections:

....

....

....

....

....

....

JOURNAL PROMPT

I make time for relaxation in my day.

Relaxation time is one of the best ways to open up channels to messages from the Divine. What is one thing you can do, based on the card you draw, to make relaxation time more intentional?

DATE .... TIME ....

MY CARD ....

CARD TYPE
○ Major Arcana   ○ Minor Arcana

CARD POSITION
○ Upright   ○ Reversed

What feelings came up when I pulled this card?

....
....

What elements of the card's meaning resonate with me and this prompt?

....
....

Which deck did I use? What artwork spoke to me?

....
....

My prompt response and reflections:

....
....
....
....
....
....
....

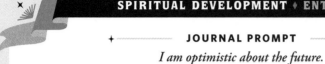

JOURNAL PROMPT

I am optimistic about the future.

Journal about the following question: "What do I believe would make the world a better place?" Use the card you draw to determine the active role you can play in creating that reality.

DATE .... TIME ....

MY CARD ....

CARD TYPE
○ Major Arcana ○ Minor Arcana

CARD POSITION
○ Upright ○ Reversed

What feelings came up when I pulled this card?

....
....

What elements of the card's meaning resonate with me and this prompt?

....
....

Which deck did I use? What artwork spoke to me?

....
....

My prompt response and reflections:

....
....
....
....
....
....
....

I create my reality with my words, thoughts, and beliefs.

The words you say out loud, write down, and repeat in your own mind have enormous power. You have the ability to shift your consciousness and manifest your desires. Start by crafting your own personalized mantra, using one of the keywords of the card you draw. Repeat it over the course of your day or week.

DATE .... TIME ....

MY CARD ....

CARD TYPE
O Major Arcana   O Minor Arcana

CARD POSITION
O Upright   O Reversed

What feelings came up when I pulled this card?

....
....

What elements of the card's meaning resonate with me and this prompt?

....
....

Which deck did I use? What artwork spoke to me?

....
....

My prompt response and reflections:

....
....
....
....
....
....

+ ---------- **JOURNAL PROMPT** ---------- +

I acknowledge both the light and dark parts of myself.

One of the easiest ways to discover your shadow side (the parts of yourself that you often view as "bad" or shameful) is to consider something that annoys or upsets you about another person. Often those feelings are discarded parts of your own personality that you have "disowned." How can you confront your shadow side, using the wisdom of the tarot card you draw?

DATE .... TIME ....

MY CARD ....

CARD TYPE
○ Major Arcana   ○ Minor Arcana

CARD POSITION
○ Upright   ○ Reversed

What feelings came up when I pulled this card?

....
....

What elements of the card's meaning resonate with me and this prompt?

....
....

Which deck did I use? What artwork spoke to me?

....
....

My prompt response and reflections:

....
....
....
....
....
....

JOURNAL PROMPT

I am my own person with my own heart and mind.

Reflect on the following question: "What do others believe that I don't hold to be true but keep silent about?" Now draw a card and consider what it says about expressing yourself more authentically.

DATE .... TIME ....

MY CARD ....

CARD TYPE
○ Major Arcana   ○ Minor Arcana

CARD POSITION
○ Upright   ○ Reversed

What feelings came up when I pulled this card?

....

....

What elements of the card's meaning resonate with me and this prompt?

....

....

Which deck did I use? What artwork spoke to me?

....

....

My prompt response and reflections:

....

....

....

....

....

....

....

....

+ ───── **JOURNAL PROMPT** ───── +

I am a loving being made by and from the Universe.

Based on the associations of the card you draw, what element—
fire, air, earth, or water—can you most learn from or embody right
now? (See Part 3 to learn about the elements of the four suits.)

DATE .... TIME ....

MY CARD ....

CARD TYPE
○ Major Arcana ○ Minor Arcana

CARD POSITION
○ Upright ○ Reversed

What feelings came up when I pulled this card?

....

....

What elements of the card's meaning resonate with me and this prompt?

....

....

Which deck did I use? What artwork spoke to me?

....

....

My prompt response and reflections:

....

....

....

....

....

....

....

....

....

JOURNAL PROMPT

I value time with myself.

Do you believe there is a difference between loneliness and being alone? What does your heart truly desire in relation to this concept? Draw a tarot card to help you integrate feelings of loneliness or isolation into empowering moments of self-discovery and spiritual practice. Journal about your process and what advice the tarot card is directing you toward.

DATE .... TIME ....

MY CARD ....

CARD TYPE
O Major Arcana   O Minor Arcana

CARD POSITION
O Upright   O Reversed

What feelings came up when I pulled this card?

....
....

What elements of the card's meaning resonate with me and this prompt?

....
....

Which deck did I use? What artwork spoke to me?

....
....

My prompt response and reflections:

....
....
....
....
....
....

+ ——— **JOURNAL PROMPT** ——— +

I am always evolving in my spiritual journey.

What does spirituality mean to you? What does it look like, sound like, feel like? How would you like it to be different than what it currently is? Reflect on these questions, then draw a card. Based on the card, what spiritual practice can you incorporate into your daily routine to build a relationship with the powers that be?

DATE .... TIME ....

MY CARD ....

CARD TYPE
○ Major Arcana   ○ Minor Arcana

CARD POSITION
○ Upright   ○ Reversed

What feelings came up when I pulled this card?

....

....

What elements of the card's meaning resonate with me and this prompt?

....

....

Which deck did I use? What artwork spoke to me?

....

....

My prompt response and reflections:

....

....

....

....

....

....

....

JOURNAL PROMPT

I am a unique spirit soul with my own personal gifts.

You have a unique purpose. Your soul has incarnated on this earth, in this lifetime, for a reason. Draw a card and use its insight as you meditate on the question "How can I best share my unique gifts with the world?"

DATE .... TIME ....

MY CARD ....

CARD TYPE
○ Major Arcana   ○ Minor Arcana

CARD POSITION
○ Upright   ○ Reversed

What feelings came up when I pulled this card?

....
....

What elements of the card's meaning resonate with me and this prompt?

....
....

Which deck did I use? What artwork spoke to me?

....
....

My prompt response and reflections:

....
....
....
....
....
....
....
....

+ ——— **JOURNAL PROMPT** ——— +

I am in constant communication with the Universe.

Reflect on a time when you felt the most connected to a divine source outside of yourself. Was it the sudden appearance of a rainbow breaking through the clouds? A song that appeared on the radio that seemingly magically answered a question? What does that moment have to show you about what may be lacking or what you can continue to cultivate in your current life? Draw a card and use the artwork to find your next spiritual symbol or message to receive.

DATE .... TIME ....

MY CARD ....

CARD TYPE
O Major Arcana   O Minor Arcana

CARD POSITION
O Upright   O Reversed

What feelings came up when I pulled this card?

....
....

What elements of the card's meaning resonate with me and this prompt?

....
....

Which deck did I use? What artwork spoke to me?

....
....

My prompt response and reflections:

....
....
....
....
....
....

JOURNAL PROMPT

Trust is important to me.

Messages from the Divine can come through conversations with other people. Use the card you draw to help answer this question: "What can I do to open myself up to trusting others more, in order to trust myself and my own intuition?" Draw a tarot card and see how you can use the symbolism of that card or one of its keywords listed in Part 3 in your next conversation. What experience did you have with that person after bringing up that topic?

DATE .... TIME ....

MY CARD ....

CARD TYPE
○ Major Arcana ○ Minor Arcana

CARD POSITION
○ Upright ○ Reversed

What feelings came up when I pulled this card?

....

....

What elements of the card's meaning resonate with me and this prompt?

....

....

Which deck did I use? What artwork spoke to me?

....

....

My prompt response and reflections:

....

....

....

....

....

+ ———————— **JOURNAL PROMPT** ———————— +

I want to live a life that is in alignment with what I believe.

Pursuing material goals at the expense of spiritual goals can leave you feeling out of alignment. However, material goals can also allow you opportunities to pursue spiritual goals. Alignment is key. What, if anything, is blocking that alignment for you now? Based on the card you draw, how can you release that potential blockage?

DATE .... TIME ....

MY CARD ....

CARD TYPE
○ Major Arcana   ○ Minor Arcana

CARD POSITION
○ Upright   ○ Reversed

What feelings came up when I pulled this card?

....

....

What elements of the card's meaning resonate with me and this prompt?

....

....

Which deck did I use? What artwork spoke to me?

....

....

My prompt response and reflections:

....

....

....

....

....

....

JOURNAL PROMPT

I am guided and protected.

Complete this statement: "When I think about [this situation],
I feel lost and confused." Now draw a card and trust that it
is showing you something that you cannot currently see for
yourself, but that the Universe wants you to know.

DATE .... TIME ....

MY CARD ....

CARD TYPE
○ Major Arcana   ○ Minor Arcana

CARD POSITION
○ Upright   ○ Reversed

What feelings came up when I pulled this card?

....

....

What elements of the card's meaning resonate with me and this prompt?

....

....

Which deck did I use? What artwork spoke to me?

....

....

My prompt response and reflections:

....

....

....

....

....

....

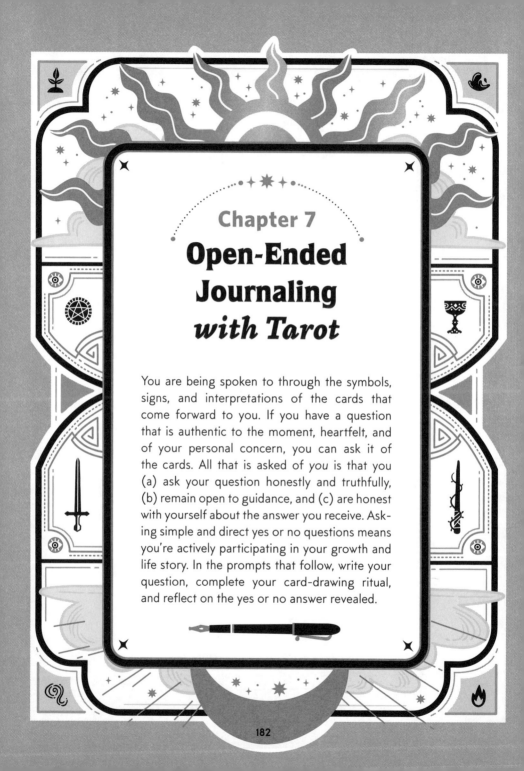

Chapter 7
Open-Ended Journaling
with Tarot

You are being spoken to through the symbols, signs, and interpretations of the cards that come forward to you. If you have a question that is authentic to the moment, heartfelt, and of your personal concern, you can ask it of the cards. All that is asked of *you* is that you (a) ask your question honestly and truthfully, (b) remain open to guidance, and (c) are honest with yourself about the answer you receive. Asking simple and direct yes or no questions means you're actively participating in your growth and life story. In the prompts that follow, write your question, complete your card-drawing ritual, and reflect on the yes or no answer revealed.

✦ ─── MY QUESTION ─── ✦

....

....

....

DATE .... TIME ....

MY CARD ....

CARD TYPE
○ Major Arcana ○ Minor Arcana

CARD POSITION
○ Upright ○ Reversed

DECK USED ....

My reflections:

....

....

....

....

....

....

....

....

....

....

....

....

....

....

....

....

....

MY QUESTION

....
....
....

DATE .... TIME ....

MY CARD ....

CARD TYPE
O Major Arcana   O Minor Arcana

CARD POSITION
O Upright   O Reversed

DECK USED ....

My reflections:

....
....
....
....
....
....
....
....
....
....
....
....
....
....
....
....
....
....

✛ ——— MY QUESTION ——— ✛

....

....

....

DATE .... TIME ....

MY CARD ....

CARD TYPE   CARD POSITION
O Major Arcana   O Minor Arcana   O Upright   O Reversed

DECK USED ....

My reflections:

....

....

....

....

....

....

....

....

....

....

....

....

....

....

....

....

....

+ ———— **MY QUESTION** ———— +

....

....

....

DATE .... TIME ....

MY CARD ....

CARD TYPE
○ Major Arcana   ○ Minor Arcana

CARD POSITION
○ Upright   ○ Reversed

DECK USED ....

My reflections:

....

....

....

....

....

....

....

....

....

....

....

....

....

....

....

....

✦ ———————— **MY QUESTION** ———————— ✦

DATE .... TIME ....

MY CARD ....

CARD TYPE
○ Major Arcana   ○ Minor Arcana

CARD POSITION
○ Upright   ○ Reversed

DECK USED ....

My reflections:

+ ———— MY QUESTION ———— +

DATE .... TIME ....

MY CARD ....

CARD TYPE
O Major Arcana   O Minor Arcana

CARD POSITION
O Upright   O Reversed

DECK USED ....

My reflections:

— MY QUESTION —

DATE .... TIME ....

MY CARD ....

CARD TYPE
○ Major Arcana   ○ Minor Arcana

CARD POSITION
○ Upright   ○ Reversed

DECK USED ....

My reflections:

✦ ———————— **MY QUESTION** ———————— ✦

....

....

....

DATE .... TIME ....

MY CARD ....

CARD TYPE   CARD POSITION
O Major Arcana   O Minor Arcana   O Upright   O Reversed

DECK USED ....

My reflections:

....

....

....

....

....

....

....

....

....

....

....

....

....

....

....

....

✦ ———— **MY QUESTION** ———— ✦

....

....

....

DATE .... TIME ....

MY CARD ....

CARD TYPE | CARD POSITION
○ Major Arcana   ○ Minor Arcana | ○ Upright   ○ Reversed

DECK USED ....

My reflections:

....

....

....

....

....

....

....

....

....

....

....

....

....

....

....

....

— MY QUESTION —

....

....

....

DATE .... TIME ....

MY CARD ....

CARD TYPE
O Major Arcana   O Minor Arcana

CARD POSITION
O Upright   O Reversed

DECK USED ....

My reflections:

....

....

....

....

....

....

....

....

....

....

....

....

....

....

....

....

....

....

MY QUESTION

....

....

....

DATE .... TIME ....

MY CARD ....

CARD TYPE   CARD POSITION
O Major Arcana   O Minor Arcana   O Upright   O Reversed

DECK USED ....

My reflections:

....

....

....

....

....

....

....

....

....

....

....

....

....

....

....

....

....

─────── ✦ **MY QUESTION** ─────── ✦

....
....
....

DATE .... TIME ....

MY CARD ....

CARD TYPE   CARD POSITION
○ Major Arcana   ○ Minor Arcana   ○ Upright   ○ Reversed

DECK USED ....

My reflections:

....
....
....
....
....
....
....
....
....
....
....
....
....
....
....
....

✦ ———— **MY QUESTION** ———— ✦

DATE .... TIME ....

MY CARD ....

CARD TYPE
○ Major Arcana   ○ Minor Arcana

CARD POSITION
○ Upright   ○ Reversed

DECK USED ....

My reflections:

MY QUESTION

DATE .... TIME ....

MY CARD ....

CARD TYPE
○ Major Arcana   ○ Minor Arcana

CARD POSITION
○ Upright   ○ Reversed

DECK USED ....

My reflections:

MY QUESTION

....

....

....

DATE .... TIME ....

MY CARD ....

CARD TYPE
O Major Arcana   O Minor Arcana

CARD POSITION
O Upright   O Reversed

DECK USED ....

My reflections:

+ ──────── **MY QUESTION** ──────── +

DATE .... TIME ....

MY CARD ....

CARD TYPE | CARD POSITION
O Major Arcana   O Minor Arcana | O Upright   O Reversed

DECK USED ....

My reflections:

✦ ——————— **MY QUESTION** ——————— ✦

....

....

....

DATE .... TIME ....

MY CARD ....

CARD TYPE   CARD POSITION
○ Major Arcana   ○ Minor Arcana   ○ Upright   ○ Reversed

DECK USED ....

My reflections:

....

....

....

....

....

....

....

....

....

....

....

....

....

....

....

....

....

✦ ──────── **MY QUESTION** ──────── ✦

....
....
....

DATE .... TIME ....

MY CARD ....

CARD TYPE   CARD POSITION
○ Major Arcana   ○ Minor Arcana   ○ Upright   ○ Reversed

DECK USED ....

My reflections:

....
....
....
....
....
....
....
....
....
....
....
....
....
....
....
....
....
....

MY QUESTION

....
....
....

DATE .... TIME ....

MY CARD ....

CARD TYPE   CARD POSITION
O Major Arcana   O Minor Arcana   O Upright   O Reversed

DECK USED ....

My reflections:

....
....
....
....
....
....
....
....
....
....
....
....
....
....
....
....

MY QUESTION

....

....

....

DATE .... TIME ....

MY CARD ....

CARD TYPE
○ Major Arcana   ○ Minor Arcana

CARD POSITION
○ Upright   ○ Reversed

DECK USED ....

My reflections:

....

....

....

....

....

....

....

....

....

....

....

....

....

....

....

....

....

✦ ——— **MY QUESTION** ——— ✦

....

....

....

DATE .... TIME ....

MY CARD ....

CARD TYPE   CARD POSITION
○ Major Arcana ○ Minor Arcana   ○ Upright ○ Reversed

DECK USED ....

My reflections:

....

....

....

....

....

....

....

....

....

....

....

....

....

....

....

....

....

+ ———— **MY QUESTION** ———— +

DATE .... TIME ....

MY CARD ....

CARD TYPE
O Major Arcana   O Minor Arcana

CARD POSITION
O Upright   O Reversed

DECK USED ....

My reflections:

MY QUESTION

....

....

....

DATE .... TIME ....

MY CARD ....

CARD TYPE
O Major Arcana   O Minor Arcana

CARD POSITION
O Upright   O Reversed

DECK USED ....

My reflections:

....

....

....

....

....

....

....

....

....

....

....

....

....

....

....

....

✦ MY QUESTION ✦

....

....

....

....

DATE .... TIME ....

MY CARD ....

CARD TYPE
○ Major Arcana   ○ Minor Arcana

CARD POSITION
○ Upright   ○ Reversed

DECK USED ....

My reflections:

....

....

....

....

....

....

....

....

....

....

....

....

....

....

....

....

....

+ ──────── **MY QUESTION** ──────── +

....

....

....

DATE .... TIME ....

MY CARD ....

CARD TYPE | CARD POSITION
○ Major Arcana ○ Minor Arcana | ○ Upright ○ Reversed

DECK USED ....

My reflections:

....

....

....

....

....

....

....

....

....

....

....

....

....

....

....

....

MY QUESTION

....

....

....

DATE .... TIME ....

MY CARD ....

CARD TYPE   CARD POSITION
O Major Arcana   O Minor Arcana   O Upright   O Reversed

DECK USED ....

My reflections:

....

....

....

....

....

....

....

....

....

....

....

....

....

....

....

....

....

....

✦ ——— **MY QUESTION** ——— ✦

....

....

....

DATE .... TIME ....

MY CARD ....

CARD TYPE   CARD POSITION
○ Major Arcana   ○ Minor Arcana   ○ Upright   ○ Reversed

DECK USED ....

My reflections:

....

....

....

....

....

....

....

....

....

....

....

....

....

....

....

....

+ ——— **MY QUESTION** ——— +

....
....
....

DATE .... TIME ....

MY CARD ....

CARD TYPE
O Major Arcana   O Minor Arcana

CARD POSITION
O Upright   O Reversed

DECK USED ....

My reflections:

....
....
....
....
....
....
....
....
....
....
....
....
....
....
....
....

MY QUESTION

....

....

....

DATE .... TIME ....

MY CARD ....

CARD TYPE   CARD POSITION
○ Major Arcana ○ Minor Arcana   ○ Upright ○ Reversed

DECK USED ....

My reflections:

....

....

....

....

....

....

....

....

....

....

....

....

....

....

....

....

....

+ ——————— **MY QUESTION** ——————— +

DATE .... TIME ....

MY CARD ....

CARD TYPE
○ Major Arcana   ○ Minor Arcana

CARD POSITION
○ Upright   ○ Reversed

DECK USED ....

My reflections:

────── ✦ ────── **MY QUESTION** ────── ✦ ──────

....

....

....

DATE .... TIME ....

MY CARD ....

CARD TYPE   CARD POSITION
○ Major Arcana   ○ Minor Arcana   ○ Upright   ○ Reversed

DECK USED ....

My reflections:

....

....

....

....

....

....

....

....

....

....

....

....

....

....

....

....

+ ———— MY QUESTION ———— +

DATE .... TIME ....

MY CARD ....

CARD TYPE
O Major Arcana   O Minor Arcana

CARD POSITION
O Upright   O Reversed

DECK USED ....

My reflections:

+ ———— **MY QUESTION** ———— +

....
....
....

DATE .... TIME ....

MY CARD ....

CARD TYPE | CARD POSITION
O Major Arcana O Minor Arcana | O Upright O Reversed

DECK USED ....

My reflections:

....
....
....
....
....
....
....
....
....
....
....
....
....
....
....
....
....
....

+ ———— **MY QUESTION** ———— +

....

....

....

DATE .... TIME ....

MY CARD ....

CARD TYPE
O Major Arcana   O Minor Arcana

CARD POSITION
O Upright   O Reversed

DECK USED ....

My reflections:

....

....

....

....

....

....

....

....

....

....

....

....

....

....

....

MY QUESTION ✦

....

....

....

DATE .... TIME ....

MY CARD ....

CARD TYPE   │ CARD POSITION
○ Major Arcana   ○ Minor Arcana   │ ○ Upright   ○ Reversed

DECK USED ....

My reflections:

....

....

....

....

....

....

....

....

....

....

....

....

....

....

....

....

....

MY QUESTION

DATE .... TIME ....

MY CARD ....

CARD TYPE
○ Major Arcana   ○ Minor Arcana

CARD POSITION
○ Upright   ○ Reversed

DECK USED ....

My reflections:

✦ ——— MY QUESTION ——— ✦

....

....

....

DATE .... TIME ....

MY CARD ....

CARD TYPE | CARD POSITION
O Major Arcana   O Minor Arcana | O Upright   O Reversed

DECK USED ....

My reflections:

....

....

....

....

....

....

....

....

....

....

....

....

....

....

....

....

--- ✦ --- **MY QUESTION** --- ✦ ---

DATE .... TIME ....

MY CARD ....

CARD TYPE
○ Major Arcana   ○ Minor Arcana

CARD POSITION
○ Upright   ○ Reversed

DECK USED ....

My reflections:

MY QUESTION

....

....

....

....

DATE .... TIME ....

MY CARD ....

CARD TYPE
O Major Arcana   O Minor Arcana

CARD POSITION
O Upright   O Reversed

DECK USED ....

My reflections:

....

....

....

....

....

....

....

....

....

....

....

....

....

....

....

....

....

....

+ ———— **MY QUESTION** ———— +

....

....

....

DATE .... TIME ....

MY CARD ....

CARD TYPE
O Major Arcana   O Minor Arcana

CARD POSITION
O Upright   O Reversed

DECK USED ....

My reflections:

....

....

....

....

....

....

....

....

....

....

....

....

....

....

....

....

....

+ ——— **MY QUESTION** ——— +

....
....
....

DATE .... TIME ....

MY CARD ....

CARD TYPE   CARD POSITION
○ Major Arcana ○ Minor Arcana   ○ Upright ○ Reversed

DECK USED ....

My reflections:

....
....
....
....
....
....
....
....
....
....
....
....
....
....
....
....
....

MY QUESTION

DATE .... TIME ....

MY CARD ....

CARD TYPE
O Major Arcana   O Minor Arcana

CARD POSITION
O Upright   O Reversed

DECK USED ....

My reflections:

MY QUESTION

DATE .... TIME ....

MY CARD ....

CARD TYPE
○ Major Arcana   ○ Minor Arcana

CARD POSITION
○ Upright   ○ Reversed

DECK USED ....

My reflections:

MY QUESTION

....

....

....

DATE .... TIME ....

MY CARD ....

CARD TYPE
O Major Arcana   O Minor Arcana

CARD POSITION
O Upright   O Reversed

DECK USED ....

My reflections:

....

....

....

....

....

....

....

....

....

....

....

....

....

....

....

....

....

....

MY QUESTION

....

....

....

DATE .... TIME ....

MY CARD ....

CARD TYPE
O Major Arcana   O Minor Arcana

CARD POSITION
O Upright   O Reversed

DECK USED ....

My reflections:

....

....

....

....

....

....

....

....

....

....

....

....

....

....

....

....

....

Part 3

TAROT CARD REFERENCE GUIDE

While you are strongly encouraged to use your intuition and build your own personal relationship with the tarot cards, the saying stands: To break and bend the rules, it first helps to know them.

Use the following guide to understand the traditional definitions of each card and to interpret how it relates to the context of your own questions and/or situations. Refer to this part if you ever feel overwhelmed or unsure during a reading. By exploring both positive and negative manifestations of each card, you can broaden your perspective and get more creative in how you notice the cards' various messages appearing in your own life.

INTRODUCTION TO THE MAJOR ARCANA

As mentioned in Part 1, the Major Arcana consists of twenty-two archetypal cards that focus on the larger questions or internal forces we are contending with at a given moment in our lives. Together, these cards make up the proverbial "hero's journey." It begins with card Zero, The Fool, who is embarking on this soul journey as a blank slate—stepping into the unknown, much like we do when we are born, progressing day by day and collecting new feelings and experiences along the way. It ends with card Twenty-One, The World card, which represents our "mastery" of the world, at which point we are ready to start again on a new path, bringing along everything we've learned.

Pulling a Major Arcana card is a sign that the question you're asking is likely an important one in your life's journey. The wisdom of that card points to what tools and resources are available to you as you navigate this situation. In the following guide, you will find information to help you interpret the Major Arcana cards in your readings:

♦ **MANTRA** The mantra represents the main theme of the card and can be repeated out loud, silently, or written in your journal to help you embody the wisdom of the card.

♦ **UPRIGHT** When the card is pulled upright, it reveals traditional themes and symbols to help guide your personal interpretation.

♦ **REVERSED** When the card is pulled reversed, or upside down, it signals an energetic shift in the card's traditional meaning. It can indicate that there is a release of difficulty on the horizon, that you've integrated a hard-fought lesson. Or it may indicate that something in the traditional meaning is inaccessible or blocked, but that it's available to you with some adjustment. If you do not read reversals, incorporate all aspects of the traditional meaning as you formulate your personal interpretations and reflections. Every tarot pull is an invitation into every side—light and dark, positive and negative—of that card's meaning.

- ◆ **ASTROLOGICAL SYMBOLISM** This section lists the astrological sign(s) and/or corresponding planet(s) that rule this card. This information can add more dimension to your understanding of the card's energy, as each astrological sign and planet is linked to specific energies (as well as unique strengths and weaknesses). Look online for more information about the meanings of the signs and planets.

- ◆ **ELEMENT** This is the card's ruling element—fire, earth, air, or water— which also corresponds to the Minor Arcana and the suits of Wands, Pentacles, Swords, and Cups, respectively.

THE MAJOR ARCANA GUIDE

0 ◆ THE FOOL

MANTRA *"I am embarking on this new journey with excitement."*

UPRIGHT Adventure, new beginnings, originality, spirited, enthusiasm, trying something new, being bold.

REVERSED Foolishness, gullibility, recklessness, lack of planning, impulsivity, repeating the same mistakes, throwing caution to the wind.

ASTROLOGICAL SYMBOLISM Uranus

ELEMENT Air

I ◆ THE MAGICIAN

MANTRA *"My words and thoughts have immense power."*

UPRIGHT Manifestation, willpower, creativity, self-empowerment, connected to Spirit and the earth, molding, desire, harnessing potential.

REVERSED Manipulations, trickery, playing "God," controlling, crossing boundaries.

ASTROLOGICAL SYMBOLISM Mercury

ELEMENT Air

II ♦ THE HIGH PRIESTESS

MANTRA *"I trust my intuition."*

UPRIGHT Wisdom, knowledge, inner knowing, intuition, virtue, subconscious, the hidden realms, books, spirituality, mystery.

REVERSED Confusion, feeling lost, indecision, not trusting yourself, seeing hidden motives where there are none, repression, information overload, cognitive dissonance.

ASTROLOGICAL SYMBOLISM The Moon

ELEMENT Water

III ♦ THE EMPRESS

MANTRA *"I nurture myself and others."*

UPRIGHT Fertility, a gentle approach, sensuality, luxury, pregnancy, beauty, nature, the Divine Feminine.

REVERSED Smothering, lack of confidence, overabundance, laziness, insecurity.

ASTROLOGICAL SYMBOLISM Venus

ELEMENT Earth

IV ♦ THE EMPEROR

MANTRA *"I am the author of my own life."*

UPRIGHT Authority, protection, discipline, stability, determination, ambition, hard work, experience, the Divine Masculine.

REVERSED Overbearing nature, brutality, cruelty, dominance, tyranny, stubbornness, obstinacy, dismissing, avoiding.

ASTROLOGICAL SYMBOLISM Aries

ELEMENT Fire

V ◆ THE HIEROPHANT

MANTRA *"My beliefs empower me to live authentically."*

UPRIGHT Teachers, trusted advisors, tradition, beliefs, spirituality, religious institutions, wisdom, initiation, rites of passage, formal study, wholesomeness.

REVERSED Stubborn beliefs, rigid dogma, zealotry, overly conventional thinking, forced conformity, bullying from social groups, bureaucracy, acting out of alignment.

ASTROLOGICAL SYMBOLISM Taurus

ELEMENT Earth

VI ◆ THE LOVERS

MANTRA *"My relationships are a mirror of how I see myself."*

UPRIGHT Balance of opposites, relationships, choices, blessed unions, intimacy, vulnerability, trust, respect and empowerment, romance and sensuality, mind-body-soul alignment.

REVERSED Inner or external conflict, lack of accountability or responsibility, deceit or doublespeak, imbalance, one-sided relationships, fear of commitment, abandonment.

ASTROLOGICAL SYMBOLISM Gemini

ELEMENT Air

VII ◆ THE CHARIOT

MANTRA *"I am the driving force of my life."*

UPRIGHT Forward momentum, in the flow, personal drive, success and ambition, discipline and control, initiating force, victory, divine will.

REVERSED Rudderless, lost and confused, flying so fast that you miss details, not seeing the forest for the trees, tunnel vision, obsessive or too aggressive.

ASTROLOGICAL SYMBOLISM Cancer

ELEMENT Water

VIII ◆ STRENGTH

MANTRA *"I lead from the heart."*

UPRIGHT Courage and bravery, heart-centered approach, taming dangerous situations or inclinations, compassion, a gentle touch, leading by example, resilience.

REVERSED Coercion, codependence, cowardice, impulsive outbursts, feelings of shame, lack of confidence, low self-esteem, doubting one's abilities.

ASTROLOGICAL SYMBOLISM Leo

ELEMENT Fire

IX ◆ THE HERMIT

MANTRA *"I shine a light for others behind me with all I've learned."*

UPRIGHT Pursuit of knowledge, imparting knowledge, introspection, constructive solitude, contemplation.

REVERSED Loneliness, isolation, rejection, withdrawal, lack of self-awareness, outcast.

ASTROLOGICAL SYMBOLISM Virgo

ELEMENT Earth

X ◆ WHEEL OF FORTUNE

MANTRA *"I accept the cycles of life by maintaining a positive outlook."*

UPRIGHT Fate, karma, good luck, destiny, changes, making the most of good moments, happiness and abundance.

REVERSED Bad luck, delays, feeling like a victim of fate, accepting inevitability, resistance to change, trying to control what is out of your control.

ASTROLOGICAL SYMBOLISM Jupiter

ELEMENT Fire

XI ◆ JUSTICE

MANTRA *"I act according to my truth, knowing my actions have consequences."*

UPRIGHT Fairness, diplomacy, balance, harmony, justice served, truth, clarity, honesty and integrity, cause and effect, accepting consequences.

REVERSED Self-righteousness, lack of accountability, lies and deceit, an unfair outcome, injustice, lack of morality, inability to compromise, taking unfair blame or credit.

ASTROLOGICAL SYMBOLISM Libra

ELEMENT Air

XII ◆ THE HANGED MAN

MANTRA *"I surrender to stillness."*

UPRIGHT Seeing something from a different perspective, releasing control, sacrifice, serenity, graceful acceptance, repentance, waiting.

REVERSED Martyrdom, playing the victim, fighting the current, myopic, apathy, indifference, stalling a decision willfully, lack of growth, stagnation, low energy.

ASTROLOGICAL SYMBOLISM Neptune

ELEMENT Water

XIII ◆ DEATH

MANTRA *"I breathe into change, knowing that every ending welcomes a new beginning."*

UPRIGHT Changes, evolution, transformation, transition, acceptance, taking on new forms, immortality and invincibility, the beauty of life.

REVERSED Fear of change, toxic patterns, needing to let go but refusing, lack of surrender.

ASTROLOGICAL SYMBOLISM Scorpio

ELEMENT Water

XIV • TEMPERANCE

MANTRA *"The journey of my life is in the trying."*

UPRIGHT Peace, patience, tranquility, stability, taking a measured approach, testing the waters, harmony between body and spirit, moderation, avoiding extremes, staying grounded.

REVERSED Excess, waste, overdoing, overindulgence, lack of energetic flow, not trusting guidance or intuition, imbalanced priorities.

ASTROLOGICAL SYMBOLISM Sagittarius

ELEMENT Fire

XV • THE DEVIL

MANTRA *"I magnetize what belongs to me and release what doesn't serve me."*

UPRIGHT Attachment, addiction, obsession, greed, lust, material pursuits and pleasures, magic and occultism, raw sexuality, short-term gains at the cost of long-term values.

REVERSED Powerlessness; confrontation of inner fears and anxieties; a willingness to reconcile; acceptance of your shadow side; releasing fear, guilt, shame, and embarrassment.

ASTROLOGICAL SYMBOLISM Capricorn

ELEMENT Earth

XVI • THE TOWER

MANTRA *"I build my life on sturdy foundations. I allow what cannot support me to fall away."*

UPRIGHT Sudden change, shock, or upheaval; destruction; chaos; disasters (natural or otherwise); false footing or foundations; instigator; loss.

REVERSED Seeing the truth, rebuilding, starting from the beginning, no baggage, the possibility of personal transformation, spiritual awakening.

ASTROLOGICAL SYMBOLISM Mars

ELEMENT Fire

XVII · THE STAR

MANTRA *"I am both human and divine."*

UPRIGHT Healing, hope, faith, blessings, rejuvenation and reinvigoration, renewal, spirituality, sense of purpose, balanced chakras, pure intentions.

REVERSED Lost hope, pessimism, betting against yourself, not trusting yourself, not listening to your intuition, feeling like you're being punished.

ASTROLOGICAL SYMBOLISM Aquarius

ELEMENT Air

XVIII · THE MOON

MANTRA *"I am a light in the dark."*

UPRIGHT Illusions, fears, anxieties, lack of clarity, misunderstandings, the subconscious, apparitions or visions, dreams, the unknown, projections.

REVERSED Disconnect between head and heart; negative influences dissipating; bringing to light that which is buried beneath the surface; questioning your intuition.

ASTROLOGICAL SYMBOLISM Pisces

ELEMENT Water

XIX · THE SUN

MANTRA *"When I act in alignment with my authenticity, I shine."*

UPRIGHT Happiness, contentment, joyfulness, celebration, self-confidence, the truth, innocence, accolades, energy, openness, nobility, authenticity, alignment.

REVERSED Blockages, arrogance, self-centeredness, vanity, overexuberance, pessimistic outlook or depressive thoughts and feelings.

ASTROLOGICAL SYMBOLISM The Sun

ELEMENT Fire

XX ✦ JUDGMENT

MANTRA *"In the end, the person I must answer to is myself."*

UPRIGHT A reckoning, an evaluation, absolution, redemption, a spiritual awakening, finality.

REVERSED Feeling like a failure, losing sight of the truth, feeling judged or criticized, repeating the same mistake.

ASTROLOGICAL SYMBOLISM Pluto

ELEMENT Fire

XXI ✦ THE WORLD

MANTRA *"I am the master of my own Universe."*

UPRIGHT Completion, graduation, leveling up, mastery, fulfillment, wholeness, oneness, enlightenment, nirvana.

REVERSED Lack of progress, feeling like something is missing, incompletion, fear of success, false praise, undue or unearned credit, taking shortcuts.

ASTROLOGICAL SYMBOLISM Saturn

ELEMENT Earth

INTRODUCTION TO THE MINOR ARCANA
———— ✦ ————

If the Major Arcana is describing your soul's journey, the Minor Arcana embodies where, when, and how that story plays out. The fifty-six individual cards in the Minor Arcana offer details about the seemingly ordinary situations and everyday challenges you are likely to encounter as you interact with family, partners, and coworkers—at home and at play. The wisdom of the Minor Arcana can be stark and significant, especially as you know that "ordinary" situations can be the cause of great worry or joy in your life.

Like a traditional deck of playing cards, the Minor Arcana is divided into four suits—Wands, Cups, Swords, and Pentacles—with each suit including an Ace; numbered cards Two through Ten; and the four court cards: Page, Knight, Queen, and King. Each of the suits takes on an elemental property, and the meaning of a card is impacted by its numerological significance as well. (You will explore the Court Cards in the next section.)

The following guide will help you interpret the Minor Arcana cards in your own readings:

- ♦ **MANTRA** The mantra represents the main theme of the card and can be repeated out loud, silently, or written in your journal to help you embody the wisdom of the card.
- ♦ **UPRIGHT** When the card is pulled upright, it reveals traditional themes and symbols to help guide your personal interpretation.
- ♦ **REVERSED** When the card is pulled reversed, or upside down, it signals an energetic shift in the card's traditional meaning. It can indicate that there is a release of difficulty on the horizon, that you've integrated a hard-fought lesson. Or it may indicate that something in the traditional meaning is inaccessible or blocked, but that it's available to you with some adjustment. If you do not read reversals, incorporate all aspects of the traditional meaning as you formulate your personal interpretations and reflections. Every tarot pull is an invitation into every side—light and dark, positive and negative—of that card's meaning.
- ♦ **ZODIAC SIGN** This section lists the astrological sign(s) that rules this card.
- ♦ **PLANET** Every astrological sign has a planetary ruler, and this section lists the planetary ruler(s) of this card. You can incorporate the sign(s) and ruler(s) of this card, and even combine their energies, to get a further sense of the tone and energy of the card.

THE MINOR ARCANA GUIDE: THE WANDS

Related to the element of fire, Wands represent creation—life force and energy itself. Fire changes what it touches, and when Wands appear in a reading, you are called to act. This suit encourages an examination of where you place your energy—if it is constructive or destructive—and how you can harness that creative inspiration to make more soul-fulfilling choices.

ACE OF WANDS

MANTRA *"I am a creative person, filled with passion and excitement."*

UPRIGHT Life force energy, zest for life, enthusiasm, sexual passion, creative spark, new beginnings.

REVERSED Hesitations, frustrations, creative blocks, feeling uninspired, boredom, lack of action or forward momentum.

ZODIAC SIGNS Aries, Leo, Sagittarius

PLANETS Mars, Sun, Jupiter

TWO OF WANDS

MANTRA *"I have the world at my feet."*

UPRIGHT Planning, adventure, taking the first step, ready to go, taking a trip, making decisions, seizing the moment, the world at your feet.

REVERSED Equivocation, second-guessing, stalled decision-making, poor planning, domination and conquest.

ZODIAC SIGN Aries

PLANET Mars

◆ THREE OF WANDS ◆

MANTRA *"I look forward to the future with hope."*

UPRIGHT A kingdom, growth, expansion, new places, surveying, hope, looking ahead, building for the greater good, gaining perspective, reaching new heights, a responsible leader.

REVERSED A bad host, taking more for oneself than others, impatience, hostility, setbacks.

ZODIAC SIGN Aries

PLANET The Sun

◆ FOUR OF WANDS ◆

MANTRA *"I celebrate life with those who make me feel safe."*

UPRIGHT Celebrations, parties, gatherings, joyfulness, hospitality, safe haven, taking refuge, a getaway, feeling at home, fulfillment, completion.

REVERSED Instability, insecurity, unsteady foundations, inability to commit, canceled plans.

ZODIAC SIGN Aries

PLANET Venus

◆ FIVE OF WANDS ◆

MANTRA *"I allow the challenge of competition to make me strive for my best."*

UPRIGHT Competition, rivalry, arguments, challenges, conflict, strife, tempers flared, adrenaline, scrapes and scuffles, childhood games or physical exercise.

REVERSED Creative brainstorm sessions, groupthink or group consensus, avoiding necessary discussion or conflict.

ZODIAC SIGN Leo

PLANET Saturn

◆ SIX OF WANDS ◆

MANTRA *"My victories are worth celebrating."*

UPRIGHT Accolades, accomplishment, victory, triumph, recognition from others, fame and fanfare, external validation, a crown.

REVERSED Bragging and boasting, narcissistic tendencies, inflated egos, bad reputation, not accepting compliments, not receiving credit that is owed, dashed hopes, a need for internal validation.

ZODIAC SIGN Leo

PLANET Jupiter

◆ SEVEN OF WANDS ◆

MANTRA *"I defend what I believe in."*

UPRIGHT Perseverance, defensive positioning, protectiveness, protests, being territorial, struggling to maintain position, setting firm boundaries, facing challenges.

REVERSED Failure to hold your ground, not sticking up for yourself, lack of defenses, defensiveness becoming offensiveness, rebel without a cause, lack of effort.

ZODIAC SIGN Leo

PLANET Mars

◆ EIGHT OF WANDS ◆

MANTRA *"In the in-between moment of anticipation, I gain insight about what I desire."*

UPRIGHT Speed and swiftness, messages and messengers, deliveries, travel, arrivals, breaking news, announcements, communication (print, text, online, etc.).

REVERSED Carelessness through rushing, lost items, anxiety or panic, delays or blockages.

ZODIAC SIGN Sagittarius

PLANET Mercury

◆ NINE OF WANDS ◆

MANTRA *"I am strong and resilient. I can and will try again."*

UPRIGHT Resilience, trying again, readiness, physical or mental fortitude, overcoming self-doubt, a long journey or challenge, inner resolve, steeling oneself, testing one's limits.

REVERSED Weariness, giving up, lack of confidence, feeling defeated, being overly self-reliant.

ZODIAC SIGN Sagittarius

PLANET The Moon

◆ TEN OF WANDS ◆

MANTRA *"I accomplish more by not feeling I have to do everything."*

UPRIGHT Heavy burdens, too much responsibility, carrying more than your fair share, pressure, all consuming, physical or emotional overwhelm, oppression, chores.

REVERSED Burdened by an inability to delegate, being busy as a badge of honor, abdicating responsibility, lack of self-advocation, total burnout, the aftermath of doing too much.

ZODIAC SIGN Sagittarius

PLANET Saturn

THE MINOR ARCANA GUIDE: THE CUPS

In tarot, Cups symbolize a vessel for what you give and what you want to receive on an emotional level. Connected to the water element, the appearance of Cups calls you to pay closer attention to your feelings—both positive and negative—and understand how you can better regulate, express, feel, or process them in order to act in greater alignment with your ideals and values.

◆ ACE OF CUPS ◆

MANTRA *"I am a loving being."*

UPRIGHT New love, a precious gift, emotional outpouring, peace and tranquility, intuition, pregnancy and fertility, connection to Spirit.

REVERSED Feelings of emptiness, loneliness, lack of emotional fulfillment.

ZODIAC SIGNS Cancer, Scorpio, Pisces

PLANETS Moon, Mars, Jupiter

◆ TWO OF CUPS ◆

MANTRA *"I offer love to others with an open heart."*

UPRIGHT Love and romance, reciprocity in relationships, appreciation for beauty, tender emotions, sweet pleasures, partnerships, unions and reunions.

REVERSED Breakups, disharmony, discord, imbalance, one-sided relationships or dynamics.

ZODIAC SIGN Cancer

PLANET Venus

◆ THREE OF CUPS ◆

MANTRA *"I believe in the power of friendships to lift my spirits."*

UPRIGHT Mirth and merriment, joyous celebrations, jokes and good humor, fun and friendships, abundance, acceptance, enjoyment.

REVERSED Overindulgence, partying too much, false friendships, a disagreement among friends, gossip.

ZODIAC SIGN Cancer

PLANET Mercury

◆ FOUR OF CUPS ◆

MANTRA *"Opportunities are always offered to me if I know where to look."*

UPRIGHT Apathy, indifference, discontent, boredom, status quo, not seeing what's right in front of you, despondency, restlessness.

REVERSED Satisfaction, contentment, not taking more than you need, gratitude, appreciation, curiosity.

ZODIAC SIGN Cancer

PLANET The Moon

◆ FIVE OF CUPS ◆

MANTRA *"I practice compassion for myself during times of grief or loss."*

UPRIGHT Loss, grief, disappointment, regret, mourning, somberness, absence, dismay, tears.

REVERSED Denial or lack of acceptance of grief (remaining stuck in bargaining, denial, anger, etc.), or the ability to finally let go, moving on, coming out of a period of mourning.

ZODIAC SIGN Scorpio

PLANET Mars

◆ SIX OF CUPS ◆

MANTRA *"I carry my childhood experiences and exuberance with me, always."*

UPRIGHT Childhood innocence, cherished moments, nostalgia, memories, mementos and keepsakes, the past, children, first love, reflection.

REVERSED Living in the past, anxiety, not being able to let go or move on, arrested development, inability to act.

ZODIAC SIGN Scorpio

PLANET The Sun

◆ SEVEN OF CUPS ◆

MANTRA *"I appreciate all the possibilities and act on the ones that serve my highest potential."*

UPRIGHT Illusions, dreams and fantasies, overwhelmed by options, projections, vices, escapism, glamour, temptations, inability to focus, lack of discernment.

REVERSED A need to make a firm decision, need for sobriety, delusions, addictions, gullibility or corruptibility, a call to focus, turning a dream into reality.

ZODIAC SIGN Scorpio

PLANET Venus

◆ EIGHT OF CUPS ◆

MANTRA *"I know when it's time to walk away."*

UPRIGHT Leaving, accepting something is over, feeling emotionally burdened or exhausted, giving up the chase, withdrawal, resignation.

REVERSED Hanging on even when you know it's time to let go, avoiding or prolonging the inevitable, procrastination of duties, fearing the future.

ZODIAC SIGN Pisces

PLANET Saturn

◆ NINE OF CUPS ◆

MANTRA *"All my wishes come true."*

UPRIGHT Wish fulfillment, wealth, security, abundance, magic, happiness, pleasure, satisfaction, unexpected surprises.

REVERSED Not believing in magic, over-literalness, unrealistic expectations, overindulgence, greed.

ZODIAC SIGN Pisces

PLANET Jupiter

◆ TEN OF CUPS ◆

MANTRA *"My relationships are emotionally fulfilling."*

UPRIGHT Happy families, domestic bliss, harmony, family reunions, ending on a high note.

REVERSED Domestic discord, family arguments, feeling like the family outcast, not having a good role model.

ZODIAC SIGN Pisces

PLANET Mars

THE MINOR ARCANA GUIDE: THE SWORDS

With the Swords, you enter the realm of the mind, where you wield a weapon of wit, intellect, and truth to cut through what doesn't serve you in getting to higher wisdom. Tied to the intellectual element of air, when Swords appear in a reading, you are called to consider not only the objective truth but your inner truth, and to create harmony between what is and what you desire.

◆ ACE OF SWORDS ◆

MANTRA *"My words are like magic spells."*

UPRIGHT Direct communication, a clear message, writing, intellect, wit, truth, wisdom.

REVERSED Lack of clarity, inability to communicate, miscommunications, delayed messages, indecision, feeling unheard, inauthenticity.

ZODIAC SIGNS Gemini, Libra, Aquarius

PLANETS Mercury, Venus, Saturn

◆ TWO OF SWORDS ◆

MANTRA *"I am connected between my heart and my mind and act in honor of both."*

UPRIGHT Meditation, rumination, decision-making, counsel, weighing of options, connecting mind and heart, intuition and mindfulness.

REVERSED Blocked intuition, letting the head or heart lead, imbalance, indecision, easily influenced by others.

ZODIAC SIGN Libra

PLANET The Moon

◆ THREE OF SWORDS ◆

MANTRA *"I acknowledge where I feel pain, so I may release it."*

UPRIGHT Sorrow, heartache, sadness, grief, pain, heartbreak, tears, endings, gloominess, negative thoughts or emotions.

REVERSED Acceptance, moving on, hard lessons learned, refusal to acknowledge a sober reality.

ZODIAC SIGN Libra

PLANET Saturn

◆ FOUR OF SWORDS ◆

MANTRA *"I honor my body's need for rest."*

UPRIGHT Rest, recovery, recuperation, restoration, relaxation, prayer, meditation, a vigil, silence, a time away from others, finding inner peace, inertia.

REVERSED Exhaustion, burning one's candle at both ends, burnout, being forced to rest, restlessness.

ZODIAC SIGN Libra

PLANET Jupiter

◆ FIVE OF SWORDS ◆

MANTRA *"I am gracious in victory and in defeat."*

UPRIGHT Winning at all costs, exile, competition, ruthless victory, rivalries, a bitter defeat, gloating, resentment, humiliation, feeling inadequate or insecure.

REVERSED Excess of bitterness, a need for vengeance, extortion, holding a grudge or learning to let it go.

ZODIAC SIGN Aquarius

PLANET Venus

◆ SIX OF SWORDS ◆

MANTRA *"I am safe; I cultivate peace in my life."*

UPRIGHT Safe passage, a journey, leaving troubles behind, smooth sailing, navigation, calm waters, serenity, protection.

REVERSED Feeling stuck, inability to move on or let go, stagnation, anxiety about the future, disturbing the peace.

ZODIAC SIGN Aquarius

PLANET Mercury

◆ SEVEN OF SWORDS ◆

MANTRA *"Truth matters to me. Lying to others is lying to myself."*

UPRIGHT Deception, theft, manipulation, taking more than one's share, sneaky behavior, subterfuge, gossip, scheming, getting away with it, lone wolf.

REVERSED Being exposed for wrongdoing, what is hidden coming to light, a lie exposed, a truth revealed.

ZODIAC SIGN Aquarius

PLANET The Moon

◆ EIGHT OF SWORDS ◆

MANTRA *"I always have a way forward."*

UPRIGHT An impasse, feeling trapped or stuck, restriction, limitations, constraints (self-imposed or external), confusion, lack of agency.

REVERSED Throwing off a blindfold, opening your eyes, clear sight, liberation and freedom.

ZODIAC SIGN Gemini

PLANET Jupiter

◆ NINE OF SWORDS ◆

MANTRA *"I practice remaining calm by remaining grounded in the present."*

UPRIGHT Anxiety, insomnia, worry, regret, mental anguish, dread, worst-case scenario thinking, troubling conflicts, suffering.

REVERSED Fear turning into panic, feeling oppressed, depression, anger, pretending you're okay when you're not, hiding your troubles.

ZODIAC SIGN Gemini

PLANET Mars

◆ TEN OF SWORDS ◆

MANTRA *"I accept that endings, even ones I didn't want, mean a new beginning is on the way."*

UPRIGHT Endings, conclusions, betrayals, depression, disaster, awareness of mortality, a moment of reset, no way but forward, somberness.

REVERSED Trying again and again to no avail, delays, frustrations, momentary reprieve.

ZODIAC SIGN Gemini

PLANET The Sun

─ THE MINOR ARCANA GUIDE: THE PENTACLES ─

Related to the earth element, the suit of Pentacles represents resources—how you get them; how you feel when you do and don't have them; and what security, stability, and fairness mean to you. Pentacles call you to remember that abundance and gratitude are a mindset and a state of being.

◆ ACE OF PENTACLES ◆

MANTRA *"I am abundant."*

UPRIGHT Abundance, auspicious luck, fertility, a gift, prosperity, an offering, growth, expansion.

REVERSED Missing opportunities, corruption, overreliance on others, borrowing with no intention of returning.

ZODIAC SIGNS Taurus, Virgo, Capricorn

PLANETS Venus, Mercury, Saturn

◆ TWO OF PENTACLES ◆

MANTRA *"I am harmoniously in balance."*

UPRIGHT Balance, change, transitions, juggling priorities, deadlines and responsibilities, trades, exchanges.

REVERSED Feeling unbalanced, upheavals, inability to prioritize, feeling unsteady or destabilized.

ZODIAC SIGN Capricorn

PLANET Jupiter

◆ THREE OF PENTACLES ◆

MANTRA *"I achieve mastery of what I seek to accomplish."*

UPRIGHT Cooperation, collaboration, mastery, a masterpiece or a work of great value, hard but not belabored work.

REVERSED Lack of cooperation, infighting, working at cross-purposes, feeling like an apprentice or beginner.

ZODIAC SIGN Capricorn

PLANET Mars

◆ FOUR OF PENTACLES ◆

MANTRA *"I cultivate security from within."*

UPRIGHT Wealth, power, money, financial security, possessiveness, materialism, control issues, working too hard and not being able to appreciate it.

REVERSED Taking people or things for granted, hoarding resources, greediness, insecurity.

ZODIAC SIGN Capricorn

PLANET The Sun

◆ FIVE OF PENTACLES ◆

MANTRA *"I am worthy."*

UPRIGHT Financial insecurity, lack of confidence, feeling left out, scarcity mindset, lack, fears, worry.

REVERSED Financial planning, paying attention to details, preventive measures, confronting fears and doubts.

ZODIAC SIGN Taurus

PLANET Mercury

◆ SIX OF PENTACLES ◆

MANTRA *"I give with an open heart and receive with gratitude."*

UPRIGHT Charity, generosity, sharing, even exchanges, give-and-take, reciprocity, balancing scales, comfort.

REVERSED Taking more than your share, stinginess, imbalance, giving with strings attached.

ZODIAC SIGN Taurus

PLANET The Moon

◆ SEVEN OF PENTACLES ◆

MANTRA *"Reviewing my work is its own reward."*

UPRIGHT Pausing, waiting, assessment, estimates, timing, scrutiny, growth, maturation.

REVERSED Frustration, impatience, rushing, carelessness, procrastinating, belaboring tasks or chores.

ZODIAC SIGN Taurus

PLANET Saturn

◆ EIGHT OF PENTACLES ◆

MANTRA *"I offer my many talents to the world."*

UPRIGHT Apprenticeship, learning, practice, developing skills or a craft, hard work, dedication, concentration.

REVERSED Slacking off, refusal to learn, careless errors, wanting success but not wanting to do the work.

ZODIAC SIGN Virgo

PLANET The Sun

◆ NINE OF PENTACLES ◆

MANTRA *"I show gratitude for what I have and what I have earned."*

UPRIGHT Security, confidence, a self-made person, investments that pay off, luxury, appreciation of the finer things in life, success.

REVERSED Perfectionism, appearances mattering above all, feeling like there is never enough, feelings of ingratitude.

ZODIAC SIGN Virgo

PLANET Venus

◆ TEN OF PENTACLES ◆

MANTRA *"I receive blessings all around me."*

UPRIGHT Family wealth, family inheritance, generations and lineages, property and prosperity, livelihoods, plentiful resources.

REVERSED Losses, family challenges, the weight of expectations, scarcity, taking comfort for granted.

ZODIAC SIGN Virgo

PLANET Mercury

⟶ THE MINOR ARCANA GUIDE: THE COURT CARDS ⟶

With the court cards, tarot introduces sixteen personalities organized by their suits (Wands, Cups, Swords, and Pentacles) and related elements. There is a fire family (Wands), water family (Cups), air family (Swords), and earth family (Pentacles).

Court cards represent archetypes that you may encounter in your daily life or that you may embody yourself. When the court cards appear, the "role" you play with others takes on extra meaning. An important thing to note about the court cards is that, given the context you find yourself in, you could embody any court card in any given situation. For example, you might embody a direct, authoritative persona when it comes to work or career matters, and you pull the Queen of Swords in that context. But with family and friends, perhaps you struggle with asserting your feelings, and may find with personal relationship questions, the Page of Cups is offering their guidance to you. The tarot is designed to be fluid (and gender-nonspecific), and unlike the other Major and Minor Arcana, these cards are not specifically associated with a certain planet—only a sign and basic element.

Here is an overview of what each court card embodies:

- **THE PAGE** Youthful and receptive energy, usually indicating messages or messengers themselves, or children who embody that elemental spirit.
- **THE KNIGHT** The "teenage" phase, showing how you take action and how you react on instinct or impulse.
- **THE QUEEN** Feminine or maternal energy (gender-nonspecific; speaking to the mastery of your emotions, not your gender).
- **THE KING** Masculine or paternal energy (gender-nonspecific; speaking to the mastery of your thoughts, not your gender).

In the following sections, you'll find more details about each court card in the Minor Arcana.

The Court Cards: Wands

◆ PAGE OF WANDS ◆

MANTRA *"Creativity comes easily to me."*

UPRIGHT A playful youth or child, beginning a project, a young artist, free-spiritedness, a novel idea, the start of a new adventure, imagination, cheerful.

REVERSED Impulsivity, boredom, second-guessing, lacking a vision, half-baked plans.

ZODIAC SIGNS Aries, Leo, Sagittarius

ELEMENT Fire

◆ KNIGHT OF WANDS ◆

MANTRA *"I follow my vision with courage."*

UPRIGHT A young athlete or competitor, a fast car or driver, a noble quest, having the courage of your convictions, a comedian or jokester.

REVERSED Lack of passion or direction, feeling inert, easily discouraged.

ZODIAC SIGNS Aries, Leo, Sagittarius

ELEMENT Fire

◆ QUEEN OF WANDS ◆

MANTRA *"I am a creative visionary."*

UPRIGHT A performing artist, a passionate leader, an impassioned speech, humor and wit, owning your sexuality, beauty and confidence, mesmerizing, independent.

REVERSED Self-doubt, feeling physically insecure, not believing in yourself, bitterness as a result of feeling unheard or unseen.

ZODIAC SIGNS Aries, Leo, Sagittarius

ELEMENT Fire

◆ KING OF WANDS ◆

MANTRA *"I cultivate adventure in my life."*

UPRIGHT A loyal leader, a creative genius, an accomplished artist, physical attraction, strength of will, an adventurer, a seasoned world traveler, authentic and authoritative.

REVERSED Bad management, lack of leadership skills, abdicating responsibility, ruling by an "every person for themselves" mindset, a charmer or seducer, a braggart.

ZODIAC SIGNS Aries, Leo, Sagittarius

ELEMENT Fire

The Court Cards: Cups

◆ PAGE OF CUPS ◆

MANTRA *"I love feeling love."*

UPRIGHT A messenger, a love letter, a picture drawn by a child, a dreamer, an apology, first crush, a pure spirit, sensitivity, a nonjudgmental friend.

REVERSED Emotional immaturity, shyness, gossip, living in a fantasy world, lack of coping skills, fear of intimacy or vulnerability.

ZODIAC SIGNS Cancer, Scorpio, Pisces

ELEMENT Water

◆ KNIGHT OF CUPS ◆

MANTRA *"I follow my heart."*

UPRIGHT A poet, a romantic at heart, a peacekeeper, a peacemaker, a date, feeling pursued or wooed, the proverbial knight in shining armor, gallantry and chivalry.

REVERSED Feeling rejected or thwarted in love affairs, running from difficulties, avoiding intimacy, needing many partners to feel desirable.

ZODIAC SIGNS Cancer, Scorpio, Pisces

ELEMENT Water

◆ QUEEN OF CUPS ◆

MANTRA *"I welcome my emotions."*

UPRIGHT A psychic, psychic vibes, an empath, a spiritual person, being tenderhearted, otherworldly beauty, a healer, a counselor, a caring and kind maternal figure.

REVERSED Codependency, lack of boundaries, suspicion, jealousy or envy.

ZODIAC SIGNS Cancer, Scorpio, Pisces

ELEMENT Water

◆ KING OF CUPS ◆

MANTRA *"I lead with compassion."*

UPRIGHT A compassionate leader, leading for the good of all, emotional stability, healthy boundaries, a wise teacher, a sage, a spiritual leader, a diplomat, a mediator.

REVERSED Basing decisions on emotions without facts, reacting on instinct or hunches, lack of consideration or care.

ZODIAC SIGNS Cancer, Scorpio, Pisces

ELEMENT Water

The Court Cards: Swords

◆ PAGE OF SWORDS ◆

MANTRA *"I have good ideas."*

UPRIGHT A student, a flash of insight or brilliance, a savant, mental agility, great at trivia, a high achiever, talkative, a reader and writer, an important message.

REVERSED Second-guessing yourself, defensiveness, gossiping, spilling secrets, anxious thoughts, fear of mistakes.

ZODIAC SIGNS Gemini, Libra, Aquarius

ELEMENT Air

◆ KNIGHT OF SWORDS ◆

MANTRA *"I am on a quest for knowledge."*

UPRIGHT An activist, a fighter, a champion of ideas, fighting for your beliefs, a soldier, a quick thinker, ready with witty retorts or banter, striking first, speaking your mind.

REVERSED Speaking before you think, hurting someone's feelings with your words, wielding words as weapons, rushing into danger, emotional avoidance.

ZODIAC SIGNS Gemini, Libra, Aquarius

ELEMENT Air

◆ QUEEN OF SWORDS ◆

MANTRA *"I make every word count."*

UPRIGHT A pragmatic approach, using choice words judiciously, a decision-maker, logical elegance, a problem-solver, a trusted advisor, a strategic thinker.

REVERSED Ruling with an iron fist, lack of compassion, overly critical, overly self-reliant, detached or aloof, being "all business" all the time.

ZODIAC SIGNS Gemini, Libra, Aquarius

ELEMENT Air

◆ KING OF SWORDS ◆

MANTRA *"My word is my bond."*

UPRIGHT A writer, a lawyer, a person who wears a uniform in their profession, valuing order and reason, a disciplinarian, a diplomat, a person who loves debate, methodical, a big thinker.

REVERSED Overly meticulous, controlling behavior, judgmental, inflexible, intellectual superiority complex.

ZODIAC SIGNS Gemini, Libra, Aquarius

ELEMENT Air

The Court Cards: Pentacles

◆ PAGE OF PENTACLES ◆

MANTRA *"Staying curious is my gift."*

UPRIGHT A curious child, a student, an apprentice, a magician, an investment, a new business venture, a nature lover, an animal lover, a love of the outdoors, a gardener or the garden.

REVERSED A procrastinator, feeling like an underachiever, slacking off, boredom, lack of ambition, not feeling qualified.

ZODIAC SIGNS Taurus, Virgo, Capricorn

ELEMENT Earth

◆ KNIGHT OF PENTACLES ◆

MANTRA *"I move at the pace that is right for me."*

UPRIGHT A practical person or approach, a hard worker, slow but steady wins the race, a down-to-earth person, honest and dependable, an environmentalist.

REVERSED Immovable, someone who is always late, not valuing other people's time, feeling complacent, not being happy but not doing anything to change, being sedentary.

ZODIAC SIGNS Taurus, Virgo, Capricorn

ELEMENT Earth

◆ QUEEN OF PENTACLES ◆

MANTRA *"I measure value through positive qualities."*

UPRIGHT A generous soul, a nurturing maternal figure, a person who dresses luxuriously, a person of high status and regard, a natural healer, a benevolent figure, a gift giver.

REVERSED Materialistic, spendthrift, lack of common sense, showing off wealth, not valuing your body.

ZODIAC SIGNS Taurus, Virgo, Capricorn

ELEMENT Earth

MANTRA *"I radiate stability and security."*

UPRIGHT A successful businessperson, a merchant or banker, a master craftsperson, a benevolent leader, a benefactor, a hardworking pragmatist, stability.

REVERSED Greedy, self-centered, only valuing material success, unwilling to take any risks or experience adventures, overworking.

ZODIAC SIGNS Taurus, Virgo, Capricorn

ELEMENT Earth

TAROT AND NUMEROLOGY

It can feel intimidating, even overwhelming, to memorize seventy-eight individual card meanings. Luckily, the basic principles of numerology can provide a shortcut to interpretation, as each card in tarot is linked to a certain number, and those numbers have special meanings. Using card numbers in your reflections of your one card readings can also give more dimension to your reading. The numbers may appear literally as an answer to your questions, or take on a more symbolic tone to help guide you in your consultation. The Universe can also remind you of the advice given in a tarot card through the numbers you see in your daily life.

The following chart breaks down the key tarot numbers by their numerological themes.

Tarot and Numbers at a Glance	
NUMBER	THEMES
1	Action, initiation, beginnings
2	Balance, equilibrium, options
3	Expression, expansion, groups

NUMBER	THEMES
4	Stability, security, safety
5	Conflict, change, adjustment
6	Support, harmony, responsibility
7	Analysis, assessment, growth
8	Ambition, abundance, accomplishment
9	Synthesis, awareness, attainment
10	Completion, fulfillment of a cycle, full circle

◆ Putting It Into Practice: The Major Arcana and Numerology

When considering the numerology of the Major Arcana, you can also use the basic categorizations of numerology, outlined earlier, to get to a single-digit number for the card you draw. The first cards of the Major Arcana, Zero through Nine, represent the themes listed in the previous number chart. When you get to card Ten, the Wheel of Fortune, you add One + Zero, to get to One. The Wheel of Fortune is about completing a cycle, as symbolized by the number Ten, but it's also about the cycle starting anew, with new beginnings and the number One (which is also symbolized by The Magician). For each card following the Wheel of Fortune, continue to add the two digits of the card together to get a single digit for the card's numerological meaning.

◆ Putting It Into Practice: The Minor Arcana and Numerology

When drawing a Minor Arcana card, refer to the following chart to familiarize yourself with the relationships between different numbers and suits.

NUMBER	WANDS	CUPS	SWORDS	PENTACLES
1	Energy	Love	Words	Fertility
2	Planning	Relationships	Decisions	Balance
3	Growth	Friendships	Heartbreak	Mastery
4	Celebration	Stubborn	Rest	Greed
5	Conflict	Loss	Bitterness	Destitution

NUMBER	WANDS	CUPS	SWORDS	PENTACLES
6	Accomplishment	Nostalgia	Travel	Donation
7	Defenses	Fantasy	Trickery	Patience
8	Deliveries	Leaving	Indecision	Apprenticeship
9	Perseverance	Wishes	Worry	Confidence
10	Burdens	Family	Defeat	Wealth
Page	Creativity	Innocence	Messages	Fascination
Knight	Passion	Romance	Impulsivity	Steadiness
Queen	Empowered	Intuitive	Direct	Abundance
King	Swagger	Compassion	Command	Security

◆ One Word Interpretation for Your One Card Spreads

As you grow more comfortable with one card spreads, you may decide to fill in your own chart with customized keywords that you've gained through your personalized experience with the cards. Your keywords do not have to look like the ones in the previous chart. After all, tarot is about growing your intuition. You may find it interesting to refer to the traditional meanings in the previous chart to see how your meanings do or don't align.

NUMBER	WANDS	CUPS	SWORDS	PENTACLES
1				
2				
3				
4				
5				
6				
7				
8				
9				
10				

NUMBER	WANDS	CUPS	SWORDS	PENTACLES
Page				
Knight				
Queen				
King				

TAROT AND COLOR ASSOCIATION
——— ✦ ———

Just like learning the basics of numerology can enhance your understanding of tarot cards and add more meaning to your one card readings, so, too, can understanding the meanings linked to each main color.

The following basics of color association can be applied to any tarot deck you use. When you draw your one card, notice if any color(s) stands out. The artist of your deck made deliberate choices to evoke a certain mood or tone in that card, and that color(s) can—and likely does—carry extra significance for you to apply in your interpretation.

COLOR	THEMES
Red	Vitality, power, action, primal urges (sex, anger, love)
Orange	Force of will, courage, creativity, sacral chakra, determination, socializing
Yellow	Happiness, positivity, a beacon of hope, energizing, wit and intelligence
Green	Earthiness, nature, success, money, growth, fertility, abundance, compassion
Blue	Peace, tranquility, calm, serenity, communication, clarity, truth, wisdom
Purple	Royalty, intuition, spirituality, higher consciousness, grandeur
Pink	Softer emotions (love, compassion), relationships (romantic and platonic)
Brown	Grounded, earth, stability, security, solidity, practicality

COLOR	THEMES
Black	The unknown, darkness, mystery, force, the interior, power
White	Purity, innocence, unity, cleansing, rebirth, divinity, beginnings
Gold	Prestige, prosperity, luxury, resources, dignity, strength
Silver/Gray	Intuition, peace, stillness, balance, psychic abilities, secrets

CONTINUING YOUR TAROT JOURNEY

You may have reached the end of this book, but your tarot journey isn't over! While the goal of the one card spread is to gain a greater understanding of yourself and the influences around you quickly, easily, and effectively, the relationship you are building with yourself and the Universe through the cards is ongoing.

Tarot is a continuous journey of mastery: The more you learn, the more you understand that each card's history and wisdom have more meaningful layers to unfold and apply to your life. The idea of one card spreads is not that you have to "graduate" to three card spreads or the Celtic Cross or any other more elaborate spreads. You can, of course! But the beauty of this method is that it has new insight every time you draw one card. It's all based on the unique context you bring to it—and, of course, on the new you and your new perspectives that are developing and shifting every day.

So keep traveling along this journey; continue enjoying these seventy-eight guides, friends, personal cheerleaders, and confidantes.

✺ INDEX ✺

for emotional well-being, 26–51,
130–55
for family, 78–103
for finances, 104–29
for friends, 78–103
for guidance, 7, 59, 94
for health, 26–51, 130–55
intentions and, 7, 17–19, 22
for interpreting messages, 7, 17,
20–227
journal pages for, 25–227
for love, 52–77
for mental well-being, 26–51, 130–55
open-ended prompts, 7, 17, 22–23,
182–227
for personal development, 26–51
for physical well-being, 26–51,
130–55
purpose of, 20–24
for relationships, 52–77
for self-care, 26–51
for spiritual development, 156–81
topics for, 7, 22–24, 26–181
Psychics, 14

Q

Queen
explanation of, 238, 254
meanings of, 254–59
zodiac signs and, 255–59
Questions
asking, 7, 20, 22–23, 26–227, 229
open-ended questions, 7, 17, 22–23,
182–227
recording, 20–227

R

Readings
candles for, 18–19
crystals for, 18
incense for, 19

one card spreads, 11–13, 16–19,
22–24, 228–64
reference guide for, 228–64
rituals for, 18–19, 182
setting intentions, 7, 17–19, 22
space for, 18–19
steps for, 16–19
tips on, 11–13, 16–19, 22–24
Reference guide
for cards, 228–64
for Major Arcana, 229–37
for Minor Arcana, 237–59
Reflections
on cards, 7, 18, 22–24, 27–227
on messages, 27–227
recording, 22–24, 27–227
Relationships
family, 52, 78–103
friends, 52, 78–103
improving, 7, 52–77
love, 52–77
meditating on, 53
partners, 52–77
prompts for, 52–77
understanding, 52
with Universe, 6, 11, 13, 25
Rider–Waite–Smith deck, 9, 16
Rituals
candles for, 18–19
crystals for, 18
grounding methods for, 7–8, 13, 23
for readings, 18–19, 182
self-care ritual, 11

S

Self-acceptance, 15, 26
Self-awareness, 10, 21–23, 78
Self-care
improving, 7, 11, 22, 26–51
prompts for, 26–51
ritual for, 11

ABOUT THE AUTHOR

MARIA SOFIA MARMANIDES is a Leo Sun, Cancer Moon, and Virgo Rising, along with being a tarot reader, an astrologer, and an intuitive who has been studying and practicing divination for more than twenty years. Maria holds a practitioner's level certification in horary astrology from the School of Traditional Astrology, in addition to studying with, and being mentored by, many world-renowned astrologers. Maria's work in advertising has appeared in national magazines, newspapers, and billboards, and her astrological writing and spiritual-based content has been featured in *Well+Good* (where she is one of their New Age content experts), *Hey Hero*, and *Keen*. Maria has written for Astrology.com and Romper.com, and publishes daily content, tarot readings, horoscopes, and tutorials on her popular personal blog and social media accounts, found at @MariaSofia_Astro.

Jennifer Reardon

App   Attorney